STONES OF DARTMOOR
and their story

by
William Crossing

QUAY
PUBLICATIONS
(BRIXHAM)

© Quay Publications (Brixham) 1987

All rights reserved. No part of this publication may be
reproduced, stored in a retrieval system, or transmitted
in any form or by any means, electronic, mechanical, photocopying,
recording or otherwise, without the prior permission
of the copyright holder.

ISBN 1 870083 10 5

Published by Quay Publications (Brixham),
P.O. Box 16, Brixham, Devon TQ5 8LW

Typeset by Action Graphics, Westminster House,
Palace Avenue, Paignton, Devon

Printed in Great Britain by Penwell Ltd.,
Parkwood, Callington, Cornwall

Front Cover: The Langstone

Contents

List of Illustrations
1. Vestiges of an Ancient Population in the Uplands of Devon   5
2. Settlements of a Primitive People   11
3. Dwellings of the Early Men of the Moor   17
4. Crumbling Relics in a Heathery Land   23
5. With Modred and Idwallo   28
6. Resting Places of the Men of the Hills   33
7. The Narrow House of Death   38
8. Circles that Enshrine the Dust   43
9. The Way of the Sepulchre   49
10. The Pillar of Witness   54

Illustrations

Front Cover — The Langstone
1. Kistvaen, Roundy Park — 5
2. Grimspound — 11
3. Hut Circle, Grimspound — 17
4. Dunnabridge Pound — 23
5. Rippon Tor — 28
6. Eastern Whitabarrow — 33
7. Childe's Tomb — 38
8. The Langstone — 43
9. The Cemetery — 49
10. Beardown Man — 54

1

Vestiges of an Ancient Population in the Uplands of Devon

Kistvaen, Roundy Park

When summer laughs on the silver streams that wind through its silent valleys, on the heathery hills, and tors that have lost their sternness, the old Moor invites us to wander, and with a smile welcomes us to its wild domain. Across the slopes where the melting shadows of the clouds softly kiss the bracken that bows its head before the warm south wind, we slowly take our way, willing to linger, yet impelled to roam, for that which is new is ever disclosing itself, and bids us forward to look upon it. A thousand forms attract us as we penetrate into this land of solitude, and each has something to tell. But it is not Nature only that speaks. Ere we have gone far we discover that to this spot, remote and tranquil, man came in a far away time, lived here his little life, and here laid him down to his last sleep. Crumbling walls and rude pillars, prostrate and half-buried in the heather, attest his former presence. Reared in the night of antiquity, the dawn of history revealed nothing of their purpose, nor shed light on those who erected them. But in the brightness of the noon of later days much that was before obscure became visible; and though not all was rendered clear, for there is much that is still hidden from us, the sunlight streamed in where it had never yet entered. Time has taught us to understand much that was once unintelligible, and the grey stones now speak to us not altogether in an unknown tongue. A voice rises from the desert, and we listen to a story of old time.

It is impossible to walk far over any part of Dartmoor, unless it be on the central tracts of fen, without meeting with indications that man dwelt and laboured among its hills in a time long gone by. Here, in its valleys and sheltered places, are the remains of ancient dwellings and enclosures; there, rude sepulchres and strange rows of stones; on the heights, mossy cairns. Mixed up with these are remains that tell of another period. The symbol of the Christian faith uplifts itself near the columnar circle of the Pagan; the worked stones of the miner's building are intermingled with the unwrought granite of the kistvaen. Thus proofs are furnished of man's presence on the Moor in different ages, perhaps of his continuous occupancy of it. It is seen that one group of the remains scattered over the waste belong to pre-historic times; the other to medieval days, or an even later date. It is the former that we now propose to notice. To look into the dim and misty past may not be altogether satisfying, for much that we would fain learn can never be known to us, but the endeavour will none the less not be without its reward, as those can testify who have sought to penetrate within the barrier that Time has reared.

The pre-historic remains of Dartmoor may be regarded as forming two classes, one consisting of the ruins of dwellings and enclosures, and the other of sepulchral monuments. The first comprises pounds, as the spaces enclosed by ramparts of granite blocks are termed; hut circles, the dwarf walls of rude habitations; and reaves; or low banks of stone and turf. In the second may be named barrows and cairns, the former a burial mound of earth, the latter of stones; dolmens, or cromlechs as they are often called, the most striking of all the megalithic structures, but of which the Moor affords very few examples; kistvaens, or small graves formed of slabs of stone; circles of upright stones, the most important of the monuments next to the cromlech; stone rows, sometimes single, and at others consisting of two lines or more; and menhirs, or rough pillars. The blocks of which these primitive dwellings and memorials of the dead were formed have received no fashioning but that which Nature gave them.

Some of the objects here enumerated are exceedingly numerous on the Moor, notwithstanding that the spoilator has wrought much havoc there. Many hundreds of hut circles exist, and kistvaens are of frequent occurrence. Pounds are also often met with, though not in all parts of the Moor, and of the stone row, an antiquity seen in few other places, there are something like forty examples. In fact, of all objects known to the archaeologist it is only the dolmen that is rare on Dartmoor.

But at the same time it cannot be said that the sepulchral monuments of our Devonshire highlands are very striking, which is rather surprising, seeing that suitable materials were everywhere at hand for the erection of something more colossal in its character. Almost anywhere on the Moor it would be quite easy to construct a circle, or row, of imposing appearance; but instead of this we find the former not only small in size, but consisting of small stones as well, while those in the latter are often no higher than a man's knee. With regard to the rows, length seems to have been a more important object with the builders than the size of the stones composing them, so that while Dartmoor can show nothing like the rows at Carnac, in Brittany, it can at the same time boast of one that has not its equal in length in Europe. There are, however, some very fine cairns on the Moor, as well as excellent examples of the kistvaen.

But if there should be some disappointment at the comparative insignificance of the circles and stone rows — and this is the more likely as the latter have unfortunately often been called avenues, a most misleading term —the visitor will feel none at viewing the remains not connected with sepulture. The walls of the pounds are not infrequently constructed of massive blocks, and when carefully examined will be found to have been built with considerable care. In every instance they have fallen, but the stones are still piled to a height of many feet, and these primitive enclosures, seen from a point where the whole area is commanded, perhaps awaken a greater interest than the sepulchral remains, and this is not lessened on a closer inspection. On examining a stone row, or circle, the feeling is one of curiosity, mingled with a good deal of doubt; on beholding a pound, with the remains of dwellings grouped within it, though we cannot be altogether sure of its every purpose, we feel that we understand very much of it. There is a certain mystery attaching to the stone circle, but very little to the pound. A mystery may interest, but cannot satisfy us; the hut enclosures, while creating the interest, will not altogether leave us in doubt. The hut circles of Dartmoor also furnish a number of very fine examples. In the majority of instances the wall is in a good state of preservation, and in many the granite door jambs yet remain. Although constructed on one plan, the character of the wall varies in different parts of the Moor, as we shall see when we come to examine them. This is apparently due to the nature of the material the builders found at hand, and the same thing is seen in the walls of the pounds. It is possible that to this may also be attributed the small size of the stones in some of the sepulchral monuments, but that this was not entirely the case is shown by the fact that quite near to the existing remains stones much larger than those used are often found.

Before proceeding to describe the rude stone remains of Dartmoor it will be well to inquire whether there is any evidence tending to show by what people these monuments were set up, and these settlements formed. Who was it that built the huts, and the great encircling walls that men now call pounds, the ruins of which are seen in the forsaken valleys of the great waste? Who was it that reared the dolmen and constructed the kistvaen; that placed the long lines of stones on the heath, and piled high the giant cairn? What manner of men sought the Moor for their dwelling-place, and why did they choose it? It is not improbable that in the last question we shall find a clue to what we seek to know.

No one can have carefully examined the hut settlements of Dartmoor without noticing their proximity to old tin-streaming works, and while it is true that these bear proof in most instances of having been the scene of mining operations in comparatively recent times, that is no reason for supposing that they were not worked, at least superficially, in an early day. Whether the Phoenicians ever traded in the tin of Britain, as some have held, is a moot point. Professor Rawlinson is of opinion that they did; that having crossed from Gaul to the Scilly Isles they established an emporium in the latter, which they called the Cassiterides, or Tin Islands. But whether this was the case or not, and other authorities point out that there is no proof of the presence of the Phoenicians in Britain, it is certain that the Greeks traded in the tin of this country. We have some testimony of this four and a half centuries before the Christian era, for Herodotus distinctly states that tin came from the Cassiterides Islands, though he also says that he is not acquainted with them. Caesar refers to the tin of Britain, and Diodorus Siculus, who wrote nearly at the same time, also speaks of the trade in that metal, and gives some particulars concerning it. Without therefore going further into the question as to what people or peoples came to this country for the purpose of obtaining this rare metal it produced, we know that the inhabitants of Southern Britain found a demand for it beyond the seas in early times. That the Cassiterides embraced not only the Scilly Isles, but also Cornwall and Western Devon, there cannot be much doubt. It is the mainland that is the tin-bearing district, and not the islands, but it is easy to understand how the former should be regarded as one of the latter.

But it has been said that one of the results of the explorations among the hut dwellings of Dartmoor is that they show no connection with the tin works. It is difficult to understand what connection they would be likely to show. Surely it was not expected that any implements of iron would be found. If there ever were such, which, however, it is certain there were not, they would long ago have perished. And there is not necessity for supposing that because men sought Dartmoor for the ore that was to be found in abundance on the banks of its streams, they must have been acquainted with the use of bronze or iron, or if acquainted with it, that they themselves made use of it. Men may be in the so-called "Stone Age," and their neighbours in the "Iron Age"; these are not periods, but merely states, or conditions. With some of the tribes of American Indians the making of arrowheads of flint was a quite recent practice, and yet they were perfectly well acquainted with metals. Stone and flint implements have been found on Roman sites and in Saxon graves, and there are others that it is considered must have been made with metal tools. It by no means follows that because men were in the "Stone Age" they were ignorant of metals, or that they lived at a very remote period. The earliest searchers for tin on Dartmoor may not have smelted the ore like the Britons in the days of Diodorus, but they perhaps brought it to their traders as they found it, in the same manner as the Libyans probably bartered their gold with the

Carthaginian voyagers.

That there is a connection between the hut circles and the tin works is, I think, shown by the fact that we invariably find them together, not only on Dartmoor, but on the waste lands of Cornwall, and that on other waste lands where no tin is found hut circles do not exist. If we ask in what part of Western Britain tin abounds we get the same answer as we should have done had we inquired where we should look for the ruined dwellings of its early population. And on the Moor itself what do we see? In the southern part of it the tin workings are much more extensive than in the northern, and the hut settlements more numerous than important. On some of the rivers in the south there are workings practically from their source to the point at which they leave the Moor, and pounds and hut circles line the banks. But on other streams of the Moor the metal has not been found above a certain point, and there no vestiges of former settlements, or remains of any kind, are to be seen.

If it was not the tin that attracted men to Dartmoor in those early days, it is not easy to understand why they should have gone there in such numbers. It has been said that as a pasturage ground it offered many advantages over the lowlands, which were then perhaps densely wooded, and in places covered with morasses, and that it was only inhabited during summer. It is certainly true that under those circumstances it would be valuable as a grazing ground at such a time of the year, but I cannot think that we are to regard the hut clusters of Dartmoor, and the pounds with their massive walls, surrounded as they are by the monuments of the dead, as mere temporary abiding places. I look upon the Moor as the home of the men who dwelt in the round cabins that once dotted its slopes. On them the summer breezes blew, and the icy hand of winter fell. True sons of the desert they heeded not the seasons' changes, but with fodder stored, and home wants anticipated, looked as calmly on the leaden skies as they had upon the blue.

On the question of race the only guidance we have is that afforded by the names of natural objects on the Moor. But it is of all guides the most sure, for these not only receive names first, but retain them longest. Many of the tors of Dartmoor, and most of the streams, bear Celtic names, and the inference therefore is that the early people of these uplands were of that race. It is considered by some that one or more races entered Europe before the Celts, though the philological evidence does not appear to point that way. But this we have not now to consider. When first mentioned by historians the Celts are found occupying the western parts of Europe. Their language divides into two branches, the older of which is the Erse, which includes the Gaelic and the Manx, and the other the Welsh, with which the old Cornish and the Armorican is included. It is to the Gaelic, or older branch of the Celtic, that the place-names of Dartmoor belong.

And now let us set out on our examination of the dwellings and monuments of the simple and uncultivated people who once lived in our western highlands. We know them to have been a pastoral people, for the old Moor has never taken kindly to the spade, and we may be sure they were a race of hunters, too. It by no means follows that because they may have delved on the rivers' banks for tin they did not practice all the arts of the mountaineer. They shot their prey with arrows tipped with flint, used flint knives and flint axes. They cooked their flesh meat with heated stones, and drank from the hollow of their hand, or from a vessel of the coarsest pottery. We will look upon their long-deserted hearths, and upon the broken walls of their cattle pounds; we will follow them in imagination to their hunting grounds and see them return laden with the spoils of the day-long chase; we will go down with them to the river where the coveted black stones are barely covered by the turf, and we will accompany them, with slow steps and solemn mien, to the kistvaen that awaits its occupants. Come; we have far to go, and must set out on our journey when the sun shall look over Hameldon.

* * *

2
Settlements of a Primitive People

Grimspound

A silver veil of mist is spread lightly over the valley of the Webburn, and beneath it the little stream runs on unseen and unheard. On either side the fleecy covering thins out, and where it nears the steep slopes that rise from the banks the forms of rock and bush are seen like dim ghosts behind it. Above the gossamer shroud the hollows of the hills are yet dark, but the crests of the ridges are clearly defined against the sky, which is being filled with light. On one hand the hill climbs to meet a faint rosy flush; on the other it lifts itself towards a canopy of grey. Gradually the light spreads, and the crest beneath the grey is tipped with gold. Lower and lower this descends until it touches the mist clouds, which steal silently away and melt upon the air. Then in the stronger light of the new day a wide cleft in the great ridge forming the eastern side of the valley is revealed, and it is seen to be a dwelling place of man. A massive wall, the lower part of which is of stone, the upper of turf, encloses a number of rude dwellings of a circular shape, and around them are large numbers of cattle. That the inhabitants are not sluggards may be plainly seen, for scarcely has the light brightened in the sky, and when the mist yet hangs over the stream below, wreaths of smoke rise from the huts. Another day has broken on Dartmoor, and the men of Grim's Pound are astir.

This well-known hut enclosure was described in my series of articles "Gems in a Granite Setting," and has also been so often noticed by others as to render it unnecessary to give anything more than a very brief account of it here. But it nevertheless seemed desirable to commence our remarks on the hut settlements of Dartmoor with some references to it, as it is important in point of size, and is in a good state of preservation. Not so very many years ago it was apparently almost the only enclosure of the kind on the Moor known to antiquaries; at all events, those who wrote on the district usually devoted much space to it, but said nothing about the remains of a similar character to be found in other parts. It has been very well remarked by the late Mr R. N. Worth that Dartmoor archaeology has suffered from over-individualisation. Grim's Pound has been looked upon as though it were exceptional in character, instead of being regarded as one of a large number of similar objects on the Moor. While, as we have just remarked, it is unquestionably important as being a fine example, it is not more so than other pounds we shall presently mention. Before, however, proceeding to notice individual groups it will be well to offer a few remarks upon the hut settlements generally.

The clusters of ruined dwellings on Dartmoor, though sometimes encircled by a wall as at Grim's Pound, are more often found without this protection. The enclosures are generally known to the Moormen as pounds, and they are regarded by them as having been erected as cattle shelters. That this traditional belief is correct there is to my mind little doubt. The former opinion of antiquaries, that they were primarily designed as places of defence against a foe, cannot, I think, be held by anyone who will be at the trouble to examine carefully the examples on the Moor, and compare them. They are not found in situations adapted for such a purpose; instead of being placed in commanding positions on a hill, as the ancient camps in other parts of the country are, they are seen in the valleys, and an evident disregard is shown for points of strategic importance. In only one instance, that of the enclosure at White Tor, or Whittor as it is more often called, above Cudlipp Town Down, has a situation suitable for defence been chosen. In the others no advantage has been taken of the spots so suitable for strongholds that the Moor everywhere offers. With the exception named, the positions chosen would be untenable in case of attack. That a strong position would not perhaps be deemed of vital importance by the early dwellers on the Moor, whose only long-distance weapons were slings or bows, we can very well believe, but it is hardly conceivable that they would altogether disregard such an advantage if their enclosures were intended to serve as forts. But they even rushed to the opposite extreme, and invariably built their huts and surrounding walls in spots where they could be overlooked by an attacking party. Had the possibility of the enclosure being needed for defence against an enemy been anything more than remote we should surely not have seen this. It was shelter that the builders of these enclosures had chiefly in view, not points of strategic value. Nor can it be said that the consideration of a water supply prevented choice being made of tors or hills for the sites of these enclosures, for, except in one or two instances, we do not find that they possess such supply where they are now placed. They are near water, of course, and so they might have been had they been formed on spots more suited for the erection of strongholds.

It is also to be observed that these pounds sometimes occur in groups of two or three, and there are instances in which they are so close that a part of the encircling wall is common to two. Where this is so no means of communication between them seems to have existed, and we should hardly find this to be the case had defence against a foe been the object of their erection.

In some remarks on the pounds of Dartmoor in the "Western Antiquary," which were written about 1889, I pointed out that in many instances where much labour had evidently been expended on the building of the wall a large proportion of the dwellings were to be found on the outside of it, and I also spoke of having examined more than one pound in which there were no remains of any huts whatever. It is evident that in those cases at least the primary object of the wall was not that of protecting the huts from a foe. It is now considered by some that they were places of refuge to which members of a tribe might flock on the approach of a foe, and that they may have been used as shelters in such circumstances nobody will deny. The early inhabitants of Dartmoor would, no doubt, be as desirous of entrenching themselves behind good stone walls in a case of absolute danger as the people of Islington were when they feared meeting with the mad dog of Goldsmith's elegy. Any port in a storm, and to be pent up for a short time in a cattle pound was better than being laid low by a flint axe. But the experience must have been far from pleasing when they looked forth and saw the enemy despoiling the houses they had foolishly built outside the wall instead of inside of it. No; the pounds of Dartmoor were never put to such a use very often, or we should not have seen the existing state of things.

That in certain instances the possibility of the necessity arising for a place where all might gather for safety was kept in view when a pound was built may very well be believed. But it is not what may have been the case with regard to a few, but what was the original and general intention of them, and that this was to shelter the cattle of the settlers from beasts of prey at night seems to me the only reasonable explanation of them. It is very pleasing to picture the hut pounds of the Moor as strongholds of the "fierce Daumonian warrior," and many will be inclined to pardon his ignorance of fortification, and his crass stupidity in leaving more than half his dwellings unprotected, for the sake of the poetry that clings to him, and will be loth to change his fortress for a cattle-fold. But the men who went to Dartmoor found something better to do than throw flints at one another. They discovered that in that upland region the summer pasturage was good, and so they became herdsmen, and built shelters for their beasts to protect them alike from the snows of winter and from ravening wolves.

It has been suggested that a wall so large as that seen in some of the pounds would hardly have been necessary if its purpose was only that of confining cattle. This is perfectly true; such a massive wall would not be required if it had been possible to carry a narrower one to the desired height. The material employed in its construction was the surface granite of the Moor; the men who laid the blocks in their courses were unprovided with tools, and no mortar of any kind was used. A dry wall, particularly if it be built of rough, unsquared stones, cannot be carried very high unless the base be of considerable width. It is probable that the walls of most of the Dartmoor pounds were formed of two parallel walls of stone, placed a few feet apart, the space between being filled with turf. This was perhaps raised to a man's height, and above that rose another wall of turf. To compare small things with great, they were built on the same plan as the mighty rampart that surrounded Babylon. The stone faces of the wall were, no doubt, inclined inward, or "battered," as a builder would say. In the lapse of ages the turf has been washed away by the rains, and the stones have fallen. In a few examples the lower course is still to be seen, but beyond this the wall of the Dartmoor hut enclosures is now nothing more than a confused heap of granite blocks.

For the most part the pounds of Dartmoor are roughly circular in shape. They vary considerably in size, some of the larger examples covering a space of three or four acres, and even more, while others are not above half that extent, and a few are so small as to render the supposition probable that they were designed for the purpose of securing a few beasts in only, or perhaps a single one, which it may have been desired to separate from the herd. The area of Grim's Pound is about four acres, and it is consequently very nearly the largest on the Moor.

Sometimes small enclosures are seen within the pounds, and are formed by a low wall springing off from the main one, and encircling a space perhaps two or three times as large as a hut circle. Examples of these little courts may be seen at Grim's Pound. They were, perhaps, used for the same purpose as the diminutive pounds just referred to.

The situation of Grim's Pound is such as to render it better known than perhaps any similar enclosure on the Moor. Thirty years ago a road was cut from the Princetown and Moreton highway to the lower part of the valley of Challacombe, and this runs so close to the ancient hut cluster that the visitor is now able to drive almost to its wall. The distance from Moreton is about six miles, and from Two Bridges nine miles. During summer there are coach trips through the valley.

The hut circles at Grim's Pound are not such fine examples as are met with in some other settlements on the Moor, but they preserve the general characteristics nevertheless. The wall of one of them was restored a few years ago, in order that the visitor might gain a better idea of the form and arrangement of these rude dwellings than is possible from a brief examination of their ruins, but this has lately been destroyed by an act of vandalism. In order that it might not be injured by cattle, it was protected by an iron fencing, and its preservation was thought to be assured. But unfortunately this proved no obstacle to those bent on damaging an object which others found a pleasure in looking upon, and another proof is afforded of what the spirit of mischief will do when the absence of brains gives it sufficient room for exercise. Eighty years ago Carrington sung of the "Crawling Cad" on Dartmoor. We may not hear of so much crawling now, but that he is present there sometimes is evident.

With regard to the question of early tin mining on the Moor, it must not be overlooked that this important hut settlement is situated in the midst of the chief tin-bearing district within its confines. Quite close to Grim's Pound are the Vitifer Mines, where old workings are most extensive, and where operations are still in progress. Whether we believe the one to have been associated with the other or not, the fact remains that on the ground where man evidently found, and still finds, tin in unusual abundance, there is seen that one of his walled settlements, which is generally regarded as being of more than ordinary importance. The late Mr C. Spence Bate was, indeed, of opinion that the tin was stored within the pounds; that the latter were in fact intended as places in which it might be placed in security. That those who procured the ore from the banks of the streams brought it to their huts to keep until such time as they were able to dispose of it, it is of course only reasonable to suppose; but that the intention of the great encircling wall was to form a place in which it might be stored cannot, I think, be seriously entertained.

Few stories attach to the pounds of Dartmoor, and Grim's Pound does not appear to be more celebrated in tradition than the others. The only story that I have been able to gather concerning it is one that I heard on the Moor in 1874, and which I have reason to believe is simply an invention to account for the name. It was said that the pound was miraculously erected by a dwarf called Grimgie. He entered the valley with a number of labourers, and there being no suitable dwellings for them, they grew discontented. But Grimgie bade them be of good cheer, and said that they should have habitations that would keep out the rain and the snow. Accordingly he led them one day to a spot where a number of little round houses stood ready for them, the whole being enclosed within a high bank. I could not discover in what work the labourers were engaged, but Grimgie, it appears, was very kind to them, and often went into Widecombe to fetch certain things that they required. That this, however, was very little trouble to him we can well imagine when we learn that Grimgie was in the habit of flying over Hameldon. Could this be shown to be an old tradition, the story might be of some value as pointing to the presence of early tinners in the valley, for the labourers could scarcely have been anything else, but from certain circumstances attending its narration, I believe that the Grimgie of the story is really the Binjie of Cranmere Pool, credited with the doings of a certain Jack How, a noted pixy, who once haunted the valley of the West Ockment.

As is usually the case with regard to hut settlements of the Moor, remains of another character are to be seen near Grim's Pound, but we defer our notice of these until we come to describe the class of monumemts to which they belong. Not far distant, too, are other huts, and over the ridge towards Natsworthy is another enclosure known as Berry Pound. The ruined rampart of this, however, presents a very different appearance from that of Grim's Pound, and similar contrasts between other pounds are observable in various parts of the moor.

As we have already observed, the choice of the material of which the walls of these pounds were formed was dictated by the size and quantity of the stones covering the ground chosen as their sites. If they were large, as in the combe between Hameldon and Hookney Tor, or on Hickaton Hill and Brown Heath, the wall was, of course, formed of them, and so their ruins now exhibit blocks of enormous size heaped one upon the other. But if the surface stones were small, no attempt was made to bring larger ones from a distance; the builder used whatever came to hand, and the result was a wall such as that to be seen in the pounds near Yealm Head. When the stones were found in large numbers it is also probable that the wall was carried higher than when they were scarce.

Not only are hut settlements of much less frequent occurence in the northern part of Dartmoor than in the southern, as we have mentioned, but walled clusters are almost unknown there. If we would see these we must go to the valley of the Avon, the Red Brook, the Glaze, the Erme, and the Yealm, not to the banks of the Tavy, the Ockments, or the Taw. As tin was abundant in the former streams, but was apparently comparatively rare in the latter this might be thought to be an argument in favour of Mr Spence Bate's contention that the pounds were tin stores; it is certainly a fact that goes a long way to show that they were the abodes of men interested in streaming for it.

But the sun is now looking down upon the combe where the great wall encircles the huts, and as we mount the hill to the southward we share the view with him. Men are driving cattle from the enclosure, and already a number are passing up the slope to the open Moor. Presently we hear the barking of dogs, and then from some of the small round buildings horses are brought forth. Three or four of the men, of the apparently better conditioned sort, spring on their backs, and with loud shouts approach the entrance to the pound. Others follow them on foot, and they stream through the gateway, and begin to climb the shoulder of Hameldon towards where we stand. As they pass us by we notice that they are dressed in the skins of beasts, and that some wear ornaments in the form of long strings of the teeth of animals. They carry flint axes, and some boar spears with polished flint heads. They sweep by us, and almost before we are aware of it they are gone. We listen; and by and bye the deep baying of the dogs is heard. The exultant shouts arise, and we know that in the bush that fills the bottom of the valley the hunters have found their prey. Ere long the baying becomes more faint, and the cries of the men gradually die away. We hasten to the summit of the hill, but they are gone. Nothing meets our view across rocky tor and distant forest. We turn our faces towards the valley through which the Dart comes singing from its mountain home, for our way lies beyond it to a humbler stream that men call the Mardle.

3
Dwellings of the Early Men of the Moor

Hut Circle, Grimspound

When the men who found their way to Dartmoor in the days that are dim set about building habitations for themselves, they were put to no trouble to obtain the materials wherewith to construct them. Granite for the walls there was in abundance, and heather, with, in many parts, rushes, for the roofs. Poles for supporting these had in some instances, perhaps, to be brought from a distance, though there is little doubt that dwarf oaks and other trees grew in many of the river valleys, and were to be seen there far into historic times, when they afforded harbour for the red deer that were hunted by the Saxon and Norman Kings. All that was necessary was at hand, and the site having been chosen, the dwellings soon sprang up. The years rolled on, and then it came about that those whom they had sheltered deserted them. Then all that was perishable soon fell to decay, but such parts of them as were built of the

17

enduring granite of the Moor the tempests of the centuries have been unable to injure, and they are here for us to look upon to-day.

The remains of these dwellings, to which the name of hut circles has been given, are distinguishable at a glance from the sepulchral circle. The latter is composed of stones set in the ground a short distance apart, usually a few feet, while in the former these are placed close together, and are generally of a different form from those of the sepulchral circle, as will be seen when we come to notice some examples of the latter. In size the hut circles vary considerably, some being no more than about ten feet in diameter, measured on the inside, while others are as much as twenty-nine or thirty feet. The average size, however, is from eighteen to twenty-four feet.

We have already said that the walls of these ancient huts are not all constructed in the same manner, and that this is probably due to the nature of the material obtainable. Of course, dwellings of this kind may have been built on Dartmoor during a period of many centuries, and probably were, and there would be nothing surprising if the lapse of time brought certain modifications. But if the difference in the mode of construction was attributable to this, we should see the several kinds of walls in various parts of the Moor. This, however, we do not. It is only in a few places that the usual manner of building them is departed from, and where these instances are met with an examination of the surroundings will reveal a sufficient reason for this having been done. The wall is generally found to be formed of stones set on their edges in the ground, and is from two to four feet in height. As a rule, these stones are not particularly large, though there are exceptions; near the road leading from the highway to Grim's Pound are a few hut circles in which some massive slabs are to be seen. Sometimes the wall, instead of being formed in this manner, has the stones composing it laid in courses, and in a few examples the greater part of the wall consists of turf. When this is the case it is wider than usual, and in some examples noticed further on this is as much as seven or eight feet, and even more. In these the wall consists of two concentric circles of stone, the space between them being filled with earth. But this is altogether exceptional, slabs of granite being in most instances the only material used. The interstices were, of course, filled with turf, and this was also no doubt laid on the stones to give the wall a level surface.

The entrance to these circular dwellings generally faces the south, and in some of the best examples the rude door-jambs — slabs placed at right angles to those in the wall — are still to be seen. In rare instances the entrance is sheltered by a wall, which, springing from one side of it, is carried round in front, so as to form a short passage, which when roofed in served as a porch. It is not unusual to find the walls of these huts in such a ruinous condition that all traces of the entrance are lost, and measurements of them are impossible. But while this is so, there are few clusters that do not afford examples where their form and mode of construction can be studied.

The absence of stone within the hut circles proves that none was employed in the support of the roof, posts being no doubt used for that purpose. A few loose fragments, or small blocks, are sometimes seen on which those may have rested, and there are also instances in which a wall runs across the interior of the hut, which, though the evident intention of it was to form two chambers, would, of course, also act as a support for the roof. The latter was formed of poles, laid on the wall, and converging to a point, and on these was placed a covering of thatch. It is probable that the roof did not slope very much, for regard would have to be paid to the winter storms of the Moor. The appearance of these early dwellings was therefore that of low, round cabins, the wall of which was not more than three or four feet in height, and the apex of the roof not above six or seven. The doorway, which was protected by a curtain of skins, could only be entered by stooping, but within the ground was excavated, and this gave additional height to the hut.

That any of the early dwellings on Dartmoor were of the so-called beehive type is not apparent from the existing remains, thought it is said that one of this kind formerly existed at Archeton. There are several very small erections, only one, however, being in a good state of preservation, that exhibit this form of roof, but these probably belong to a much later date than the hut circles. The walls were domed over until they met in the manner of the larger ancient Pictish buildings, so that the little hut was formed entirely of stone. They are invariably found quite close to the stream works, and were probably built by the medieval tinners. The only prefect example is situated on the bank of a little feeder of the Erme, on Stall Moor. It is known in the neighbourhoood as Smugglers's Hole, and is usually regarded as having been a hiding-place for illicit spirits in the days when customers for cognac duty free were to be found in every parish.

The sympathetic examination of hut circles in different parts of Dartmoor during recent years has proved of considerable service. Much long hidden beneath the turf the spade has revealed, and objects have come to light that these ruined dwellings had not before been known to yield. To this work, valuable as aiding to dispel the mist that shrouds the manners of the early men of the Moor, the Rev. S. Baring-Gould, Mr Robert Burnard, and the Rev. I. K. Anderson have devoted much time, and their researches have been carefully and skilfully conducted. Pot boilers, or pebbles used in cooking, and showing the action of fire, together with bone ashes and fragments of wood charcoal, have been found, as well as flint flakes and cores, and, though rarely, pieces of rude pottery. What was evidently the bed-place has also been unearthed, and the hearth, formed of a flat stone, with the remains of back and sides, has likewise been discovered. The former consists of a row of stones cutting off a segment of the circular wall, and this is raised a little higher than the floor of the hut. On this dais were probably laid dried ferns or heather, and thus the inmates were furnished with a comfortable couch — one such as the benighted wanderer, lost on the Moor, would now hail with joy. Of course, these internal arrangements have not been discovered in the whole of the huts examined, nor is it to be expected that this should be so. A very large number of them were in all probability not dwellings, but buildings in which cattle were housed. That they were all built on one plan says nothing. We do the same thing to-day, the only difference being that our houses and cattle shelters are rectangular, while those of the primitive people of Dartmoor were circular. Ours are more comfortable, but his were decidedly more picturesque. But comforts of a sort were not lacking even with him; for when the entrance to his cabin had been secured for the night, and the fire had diffused its warmth, the hardy man of the hills could rest at ease, and bid defiance to the howling blast and the snow that buried the sere bracken and the dull seas of heather without.

Dartmoor is no longer haunted by the pixies, and we are consequently unable to ask the little elves to spirit us to different parts of the Moor. It is sometimes said, too, that the present age is lacking in imagination, both of which things are unfortunate for our present purpose. But we will nevertheless make an endeavour to transport ourselves in fancy across the waste, and as we have come with ease from Grim's Pound to the Mardle, there is no reason why, when the time arrives for us to do so, we should not continue our journey with equal facility.

The Mardle is a small stream rising on the boundary of the Forest, and it runs for about a mile in an easterly direction. It then turns to the south-east, and a mile and a half further on leaves the Moor, afterwards falling into the Dart near Buckfastleigh. Not far from its source it is crossed by a track at Hapstead Ford, and about a quarter of a mile below this, on its right or southern bank, is a large circular pound, sometimes known as Mardle Ring. The enclosing wall, which is very much overgrown, was never of great width, and its ruins form a striking contrast with the vallum of Grim's Pound. But it is nevertheless a type of many that are to be seen on the Moor, and it is chiefly on account of this that it is named here. In its upper part is a hut circle, the wall of which is much dilapidated.

But surrounding this decayed pound are other remains of a by-gone day. Further down the stream are hut circles, and northward, on the hill of Nap, and southward on the bold brow of Snowdon, are numerous cairns. But on all the hand of Time has rested heavily, and the stones that the encroaching turf has not hidden now wear coats of moss.

It is in the glorious sunshine of a summer's morning that we look upon the happy little stream, and though we are in the midst of much to remind us of the dead past, it hardly shapes itself to our mental vision. In that pure light the darkness of other days is banished, and we see only the old Moor, and the fields and woods that roll away from its feet. The golden glow speaks of the present and the future alone; what has gone before is forgotten. But there are times, according to peasant story, when the shade of one departed visits this lonely valley. When the new moon struggles to look through this dim night upon the sleeping Moor, a woman robed in white sets out from the woods that fringe the steeps, and, guided by the brook, passes upward to the hollow where it rises. The way is rough, for the tinner has here laboured hard, and has encumbered the banks with stony heaps. But noiselessly she walks over the difficult path, until she reaches the spot where the water wells up from the earth. Then she is seen no more, but whether like the dew that drops from the heather sprays overhanging the river banks, she sinks into the embraces of the Mardle to be carried once more to the groves below, or whether she is borne away on the night wind, I know not. I can only tell you that, if tradition is to be relied upon, she appears again at the coming of the next new moon.

On Dean Moor a little stream rises called the Harbourne, which in Risdon's time was styled the handmaid of Dart. Ere it has gone far on its course it reaches a narow valley known as Dockwell Hole, and turning into this soon after changes its wild surroundings for the beauties of field and woodland. In and around this valley is a group of relics, consisting of a menhir, cairns, and pounds with hut circles, but many of the objects have unfortunately suffered at the hands of the spoilator. Deferring our notice of the menhir and cairns we shall turn our attention to the pounds, one of which we shall find on the northern side of the hollow. This approaches a circular shape, but owing to its dilapidated condition an accurate measurement was hardly possible, but I found its diameter on the inside to be about sixty-five yards. Two rows of stones run across this enclosure, one cutting off a space from the southern, or lower part of it, and the other from the higher part. In the south-west corner are the remains of four hut circles, formed of large stones, and what appears to be traces of a fifth a little further up. Outside the wall, a few yards to the east, are two more hut circles. On the west side the wall of the pound appears to have been carried out for a short distance, but for what purpose is not very clear.

A little higher up the hill is a small space, remarkably free from furze and heather, with which the surrounding common abounds. A very imperfect wall encloses this space, and within it are the ruins of two hut circles, one of them being near the centre and the other close to the wall. On the summit of the hill above this enclosure are the cairns referred to, and near the head of the Harbourne is the menhir.

Lower down the stream, and on its western side, is the Dockwell Brake, within which on a gentle slope is a pound 225 yards in circumference. The wall, which is imperfect in places and much overgrown, is composed of rather large stones, but there are no vestiges of hut circles within it.

This group of antiquities may be conveniently reached from Brent. The Moor gate at Dockwell is rather less than three miles from that place, and the pounds are about half a mile further. On passing through the gate the way to them lies by the enclosures on the right.

As already mentioned, the remains at Dockwell have been despoiled, but the damage is not of recent date, for there can be no doubt that the stones were taken from the pounds to build the wall of the farm enclosures near by, and these are of long-standing. No present-day destroyer of our stone remains would put himself to the trouble of going to Dockwell to level a hut circle or cart away a cairn; it is too far removed from any frequented road. He is generally a road contractor or quarryman, and it is the very fact that he is disinclined to go anywhere out of his way for the stone that he requires that causes him to break up the ancient monuments and attack the tors. Quite recently much damage has been done on Walkhampton Common, where several hut circles have been destroyed on the slope of Leedon Tor. Mr Robert Burnard referred to this in some remarks addressed to the members of the

Devonshire Association at Teignmouth last month, but at a recent meeting of the Tavistock District Council the damage was denied. Only last week, however, Mr Burnard visited the site, and discovered that a hut circle had been practically destroyed during the previous fortnight, and that a workman was then removing a reave, as old boundary banks are called, and which are as much objects of antiquity as are the hut circles themselves. It is pleasant to note that some good has been done by calling attention to the acts of spoilation; for the workman informed Mr Burnard he had now received instructions that he was not to destroy "rounds" — by which he meant the hut circles — but that he might still proceed with the demolition of "old hedges."

Not far below Shipley Bridge the Avon is joined by a tributary called Red Brook, being the united waters of the stream of that name and of the Middle Brook and Bala Brook. The two latter first run together, afterwards receiving the Red Brook, the place of meeting sometimes being known as Henchertraw, from a miniature gorge of great beauty on the last-named stream. Here on the right bank, immediately below the confluence, is a pound of an unusual character, which goes by the name of the Half Ring. The wall, indeed, only describes a half circle, the stream forming the protection on one side, the bank being there rather high. The length of the wall measured on the outside is is 204 yards, and the distance from one end of it to the other along the bank is 110 yards. It is about four and a half feet in height, and eight feet wide, and is in a fairly perfect condition. An opening has been made in one part of it where a path runs down to a ford. The pound is situated on the slope of a hill, there being a considerable rise from the brink of the stream to the wall. Immediately within the latter, and in the highest part of the pound, are several small enclosures, one of them being in a remarkably good state of preservation, and is evidently of later date than the main wall of the pound. There is a doorway in the north corner of it, four and a half feet wide. Adjoining this are four other enclosures, having very much the appearance of hut circles, though it is rather difficult to pronounce them to be such. There are, however, four complete hut circles in the pound, and vestiges of others.

It is hardly possible for anyone to visit Henchertraw and look around him without feeling that if there were no conection between the hut settlements and the stream works, the coincidence of the occurrence here of so many remains of primitive dwellings with their protecting walls, and of extensive mininig operations, is altogether inexplicable. On Bala Brook Heath opposite and on Zeal Hill are no less than five pounds, and within a short distance of these as many more, besides scattered hut circles. From the point where we stand to the sources of the three streams we might walk over ground where the evidences of the tinners' presence would meet us at almost every step. The workings are most important in their character, and on the sides of the valleys where we see them the ancient habitations thickly cluster.

And this is the case also on the Avon, as we shall speedily see, for to the banks of that stream, to which the great morass near Cater's Beam gives birth, our wandering steps now lead us.

4
Crumbling Relics in a Heathery Land

Dunnabridge Pound

Although time has dealt gently with much that early man left behind him on the Moor, its ravages are nevertheless too often visible. So many centuries have rolled away since he formed his settlements, and set up his monuments in its lonely places, that it would be a matter for wonder had they come down to us uninjured. Even where the vandal has not marked them for his own, we could hardly expect that the stones should be as they were when the builders had completed their task. The storms of winter have thrown down the menhir, and caused the walls of the pounds to totter and fall; the rude pillars encircling the spots where the dead are resting have been cast upon the grounds, and many of the stones in the long rows that stretch across the heath laid prostrate. Then, when prone upon the turf, the heather has discovered them, and has thrown its sprays over their faces, as though it would shield them from the blast, whose assaults they had been unable to withstand. Ferns, too, have sprung up around the grey stones, and have helped to shroud them, so that the wanderer who does not know the Moor well might pass them by without suspecting their existence.

I remember when a great part of Holne Moor was covered with heather of such a height as completely to hide everything that rested on the ground. When this was burnt several interesting objects were laid bare, including hut circles, small pounds, and reaves. The latter are indeed not only often hidden by heather and ferns, but in some cases the turf has so encroached upon these crumbling banks as to almost obliterate them. They have been sometimes called tracklines, and in two cases, at least, trackways, but these terms, singularly inappropriate to banks of earth and stone, are never used on the Moor; there they are invariably known as reaves — a word, apparently, analogous with row. That they served as boundaries or hedges is evident, and if this was not their sole purpose it is difficult to see what else they could have been designed for. When they extended for a considerable distance they may, of course, have been found useful as guides in certain circumstances, but they were never tracks in the true sense of the word. It is also possible that in a few instances, where they were carried over boggy ground, they may have been utilised as a causeway, but this would only be for short distances.

The two reaves referred to as being called trackways I have known for very many years, and have carefully examined them on more than one occasion. But I see no reason for regarding them as having been intended to serve a different purpose from that of other reaves on the Moor; that is to say, I look upon them as ancient boundaries of some kind. I am aware that there are those who will not share this opinion, but who see in these two reaves sufficient evidences to satisfy them that they are ancient roads. One of them climbs the hill of Three Barrows, in the southern part of the Moor, and will be noticed when we deal with the cairns on the summit of that eminence; the other may be seen in the neighbourhood of Post Bridge and is particularly well defined on Chittaford Down. To this one the name of the the central trackway has been given, and it is regarded by some as forming a portion of the ancient Fosseway, but upon evidence which, however clear to them, is to me very far from convincing. I might possibly be a little less sceptical if it were shown how those who travelled over it contrived to pass through Lower White Tor. If it was not intended for them to do this, or to jump, like Spring Heeled Jack, clean over the pile, the motives of the sapient engineers who carried their "road" straight into the rocks are incomprehensible. There is no mistake about the matter; the reave runs fairly into the tor, and there it stops. Possibly such an obstacle was a trifling matter to the Danmonian warrior, or his Roman successor, but it is decidedly fortunate for the modern motorist that he is not obliged to go that way. There is no sign of the "road" on the further side of the tor. Those who made it probably deemed its extension unnecessary, recognising that anybody clever enough to negotiate the huge pile of rocks would be able to find his way anywhere.

The reaves vary much in size. Some of them are three or four feet in height, and even more, and six or seven feet in width. Others are less than half the height named, and only about two or three feet wide. In some instances they appear to be of considerable antiquity, but it is probable that few are of such early date as the hut circles, while many of them are comparatively modern. On Tor Hill, above the valley of Widecombe, and not far from Hemsworthy Gate, is a large hut cluster, known as Foale's Arrishes. Here the ancient dwellings are enclosed, not within a pound, but in small spaces formed by reaves intersecting each other. In such a case there can be no doubt of the antiquity of the latter. On Dartmeet Hill, and on the slope of Yar Tor, there are also a number of reaves that are evidently very old, and many of similar character occur on Clannaborough Down, near Throwleigh. Here the reaves and the hut circles are hidden by the vegetation. There is no sign of them even when the rambler approaches quite near. It is only when he finds himself knee deep in the short, thick furze that he becomes aware that he is walking over the site of a settlement of Dartmoor's early people.

In some instances reaves serve to mark the boundary between two commons, and also the boundary line of the Forest. There is a wide reave marking the limits of the latter where it abuts on Walkhampton Common, in the vicinity of Nun's Cross; in fact, that ancient monument stands in the line of it. The one already referred to as existing on Three Barrows serves to define the boundary between Brent Moor and Ugborough Moor; and there is one running from the summit of the hill known as Pupers, which separates the Moors of Dean and Buckfastleigh. This extends from the hill to the corner of the enclosures of Lamb's Down, a distance, as my measurements show, of 2,112 yards. It runs from one of the rock piles representing the pipers, from which the hill takes its name. There are two of these, and according to the story they once played here on a Sunday afternoon, while a companion danced to their harmonious strains. Suddenly the music was interrupted, and to the horror of the latter he beheld those who were expending so much wind to furnish a suitable accompaniment to his nimble steps turn into stone. To offer to pay the piper would now be a useless formality, and as there was no more music to be got out of them, he rather unceremoniously took his leave. But he had not gone far ere he too shared the fate of his comrades. You may see them if you choose to take the trouble to visit the tor. The two pipers stand on the crest of the hill, while the dancer occupies a position part way down the slope towards the Wella Brook.

Reeves sometimes marked tinners' bounds, and it is very probable that many were formed for that purpose. They have also been adapted in several instances as hedges, and in a similar manner newtake walls, and other farm enclosures, have been built on the line of the decayed vallum of hut pounds. In this connection two drift pounds, which are of an altogether different character from those we have been noticing, may be mentioned. They are Dunnabridge Pound and Erme Pound, both of which it is evident occupy the sites of more ancient enclosures. In neither case did the pound occur singly, for at Dunnabridge a second is to be seen on the slope eastward, though very much overgrown, while quite near to Erme Pound are the fine enclosures on Brown Heath.

Among the pounds alluded to as being situated in the neighbourhood of Henchertraw there are two on that part of Zeal Hill overlooking the valley of the Avon, and one of these is particularly worthy of notice. It is placed on the brow of the hill above the Hunters' Stone, which stands by the side of the way leading from the Moor-gate at Shipley to the old quarries above Brent Moor Villa. When the hills are bare it is to be seen from near Shipley Bridge, and also from the tor on the opposite side of the valley, but in summer it is completely hidden by tall bracken. The enclosure is 360 yards in circumference, and the wall is composed of very large blocks of granite, some of them indeed being particularly so. It was of considerable width, but the stones are now much scattered, especially in one place. There are fourteen hut circles in the pound, all of them being in the upper part of it, and there is one on the outside of the wall at the bottom. It was here that Reuben Willcocks met the pixies. Forty-five years have elapsed since I first looked upon the scene of Reuben's adventure, but it has not changed since that time. Reuben, it appears, was making his way towards Brent one night, having been far out on the Moor to look for ponies, when all at once he found himself within a large ring of stones near Black Tor. While searching for an opening to save himself the trouble of climbing over the granite blocks, which in the faint moonlight he was not able to see very plainly, he heard voices, and presently he became aware that a number of little elves were swarming into the pound. Almost at the same moment that he perceived them he discovered an outlet, and immediately darted through it. But he was not quick enough. A little elf who was perched upon a lump of rock saw him, and gave the alarm. "I twit! I twit!" he cried, and throwing up his tiny cap he set off after Reuben, followed by "thousands of his mates," as that worthy afterwards said. The Brent man, instead of being pixy-led, was now leading the pixies. But he did not lead them very far. They overtook him when he reached the foot of the steep slope near the river, and pulled him to the ground. And there Reuben Willcocks remained all the night, while the pixies danced round him. When the dawn appeared they vanished, and Reuben, faint and weary, fell asleep. He was discovered by a workman lying on the ground, and on being awakened seemed to be in a dazed condition. He told his story, and probably nobody would have doubted it had not a certain circumstance come to light a few days later. Then it transpired that Reuben had called in at Huntingdon Warren on his way home, and had partaken rather freely of a certain liquor distilled in the good town of Plymouth, and which was known to have the power of causing people to "see double." On the present occasion, however, it was considered that it had also exercised considerable power in the direction of developing Reuben's inventive faculties.

The other pound is higher up the slope, but is not so important. These enclosures are easily visited from Brent, from which they are not more than about three miles distant. Henchertraw may be reached from Shipley road by crossing a field on the western bank of Red Brook to a hunting gate opening on the Moor, and following the stream upwards for a short distance.

Above Black Tor, which is not far from the pound on the brow of Zeal Hill, are other small enclosures and still further up, and northward of a tiny tributary of the Avon, is the most interesting pound on the Moor. It is known as The Rings, and its shape is rather peculiar. It is a long-drawn-out oval, slightly curved, and at one place having the wall, which is no less than 975 yards in circuit, a little depressed on each side. In many parts the lower courses of this wall are still intact, and here it appears to have been originally about ten feet wide, but the stones composing it being scattered it now covers a greater space. The length of the pound is 380 yards, and its greatest breadth 120 yards; across its northern part it is 105 yards, and at its narrowest point, where the wall is depressed, is only 76 yards. There are three entrances to the pound; one on the higher side of it, and one at each end.

A similar arrangement exists in this pound to that which we noticed in the Half Ring on the Red Brook. Extending entirely across its upper part are a number of enclosures, and there are a few also on its lower part. Altogether there are about thirty, and with one exception they either adjoin the main wall of the pound or are connected with others that do so. The exception is situated in the northern part of the pound; it is roughly circular in shape, and is 38 feet in diameter. Besides these enclosures there are about a score of hut circles, one of which, placed near the middle of the settlement, is formed of two concentric circles of stone.

One of the enclosures, some of which resemble small courts, measures twenty-two yards by eleven, and another fourteen yards by twelve. That they are not all of such early date as the pound is evident, and this is particularly the case with regard to one. It is situated in the corner of one of the courts, and consists of the walls of a small rectangular edifice, similar to those so often seen close to the stream works. The heather has not reached it, though it blooms near by, but the ivy clasps its wall, and when the spring comes it brings with it the bracken, and this entirely fills the little building until winter lays its hand upon the bright green fronds, and they become brown and crisp, and waste away. Another interesting settlement in this part of the Moor is Gripper's Pound, on the left bank of the Avon above Small Brook. Here are a number of hut circles, most of them, however, being outside the enclosure. They are situated between it and the river, and are connected by reaves, which are very much overgrown. The shape of the pound, the wall of which is only 160 yards in circuit, approaches that of a horse-shoe. Within it are two hut circles, with the appearance of a third. It is rather difficult to take correct measurements of the huts, or the wall, in this group, the whole being in such a decayed state, but the latter does not exceed three feet in height.

No hut cluster on Dartmoor is more delightfully situated than that at Gripper's Pound, and on none has vegetation striven so much to conceal. The settlement is in the very midst of a clatter; the stones that men set up to form for themselves a rude shelter neighbour the rocks that have fallen from the crest of the hill. With these mingle moss and ferns, whortleberry plants and heather, and ancient thorns. Below, the Avon sings to them all.

* * *

5

With Modred and Idwallo

Rippon Tor

The shadowy figures of two horsemen are passing up the valley of the Avon. Though they appear to be speaking we hear not their voices, nor is any sound given forth when the hoofs of their steeds strike the stony ground. They reach the tributary that comes down from Brock Hill, on the banks of which we stand amid the workings of the tinners, and cross it where it hides itself in the bosom of the larger stream. They pass us by, all heedless of our presence, and so near that, dim though their forms be, we can well note their lineaments, their rude garb of skins, and the untanned leather trappings of their stout little horses. And it needs not that we ask ourselves who these men are that move before us like the dim ghosts of the heroes sung by the warrior-band of Morven. The present is with us, we know. We do not feel that we live in the old time, but only that we look back upon it through the long vista of centuries —look back upon a certain day when Modred and his friend Idwallo made search among the hills for cattle that had strayed from the fold. To our eyes the roofless huts are things of a hoar antiquity; to those of the riders, so our fancy tells us, they are as they were more than two thousand years ago. So we follow the shades of these two dwellers in the uplands, and they shall lead us to the settlements of their brethren that we may look upon them.

Passing up the slope of Hickaton Hill, with the Brock Hill stream on our right, we reach a very irregular enclosure, within which we shall notice seventeen hut circles, ranging from twelve feet to twenty-five feet in diameter, some of them being connected by reaves, and others being built quite close together. Outside the wall, on the north-west there are two hut circles, and near by two reaaves spring from it. Adjoining this enclosed cluster of huts are the ruins of some erections of another date; indeed, on this part of the hill, mixed up with the more ancient remains, are numerous vestiges that speak of the presence here of the miner of later days. The same story that is told by the Half Ring on Ryder's Plain, above Black Tor, is revealed at Hickaton. We find that the tin-seeker, who laboured on the streams of Dartmoor in the days when mining had become an established industry regulated by the Stannary Laws, fixed upon the spots where the early settlers had reared their huts as suitable sites for his own buildings. The vallum and the hut circle of prehistoric times is at each of the places named (as well as at others on the Moor) seen in conjunction with the rectangular erections of the blowing-house type, some of which there is abundant evidence to prove are of comparatively recent date. What was deemed a fitting situation for his huts by the Briton was regarded as a convenient and proper one for his crushing and smelting houses by the miner of the modern historical period, which is remarkable if what attracted one was not sought after by the other.

This enclosure is one of a group on this hill, the whole forming a most extensive settlement, and furnishing examples of pounds and hut dwellings such as are not surpassed in any part of Dartmoor. The area over which these are scattered, and which comprises the whole of Hickaton Hill, is bordered on three sides by streams, the Wella Brook, the Avon, and the Brock Hill stream. On the first and last named of these the remains of mining operations extend from their source to where they mingle with the Avon, and such also abound on that river.

Not far above the pound just noticed is another. It is 240 yards in circumference, and contains three hut circles, each of them being close to the wall. The door-jambs in one of these are four feet in height and three feet wide at the base. One still retains its original position, but the other has fallen and is leaning against the former. Outside the pound, to the south-east, a wall much decayed branches from the main one, and sweeping round forms a small court, as it were. On one side of this is a single hut circle, and on the other there are two.

But interesting though these pounds may be we shall find the one to which we now make our way infinitely more so. It is a remarkably fine example, and as we walk over the turf towards it, and its vallum of moorstone blocks, with the walls of its dwellings, rise before us, we forget that we are approaching long-deserted homes, and almost look to see the herdsmen come forth from their ox-stalls. And when we stand within it, though the spell is broken, it is still impressive. And little wonder that it should be so, when so much that belongs to the dead past surrounds us. The pound, which is of an irregular shape, is no less than 825 yards in circumference. It is divided into parts by walls, smaller than the main one, one of which, 62 yards in length, runs across it and forms two divisions. Of these, one is again divided into three by walls that diverge from a point, but which is not in the centre of the space. In each of these four divisions there are hut circles, there being altogether seventeen, and some of them are as fine as any to be found on the Moor. In one of these, which is twenty-nine feet in diameter, the remains of a wall that once ran across it are to be seen. We have already alluded to this arrangement as existing in some of these ruined dwellings. In several examples the door jambs are erect, and, as is usual, the entrance faces the south. One of the entrances to the pound is in a very perfect state, but the wall, as is invariably the case, is now only a confused rampart of stones. In some places where these are scattered more than in others it has a width of about ten feet, and is from three to four feet in height. Between it and the pound last noticed are two hut circles, one measuring twenty-seven feet and the other thirteen feet in diameter.

The view from this ancient enclosure is particularly fine. Southward is seen a wide stretch of open country beyond the Moor, with the Channel in the distance; on the further side of the valley of the Avon is the hill of Eastern Whitabarrow; and away to the north-east Rippon Tor rises against the sky, and the rocky hills above the valley of Widecombe.

Not far from the head of the Brock Hill stream is another pound, the circumference of which is 260 yards. The wall, which is overgrown in places, is about six feet wide, and encloses four hut circles, and the apparent remains of a fifth, all except the largest being in a very ruinous condition. Leaving this and crossing the hill in a south-westerly direction we shall descend towards the confluence of the Avon and the Wella Brook, and on the slope shall find one of the more numerous enclosures in this locality. This pound is 280 yards in circumference, but the wall is not more than from two to three feet in height, the stones that composed it being much scattered. There are no hut circles within it, but on the west side, between it and the Avon, there are nine, two of them adjoining the wall. Across the stream is an enclosure on the side of Eastern Whitabarrow, but it is much overgrown, and on the southern slope of Huntingdon there are three enclosures.

My first examination of the Hickaton remains was made about thirty years ago. At that time the latest Ordnance Survey had not been commenced, and their existence was consequently known to very few. The earlier Dartmoor writers were unacquainted with them, and being removed from roads they had not been discovered by the visitor. In this brief notice of these remains I have been able to do little more than indicate their character and importance. But they will be found well worthy of attention, and the visitor to Dartmoor who desires to gain a good idea of the dwellings of its ancient inhabitants will nowhere meet with a spot where he is better able to do this than at Hickaton.

There are remains of considerable importance on the Erme and the Yealm, as we shall find, but in the large settlement we have been noticing the pounds and the hut circles present features that are not always seen, and thus have a special value. Not only are the huts in an excellent state of preservation, but we have here examples of small and of large ones. We also see huts built quite close together, one part of the wall being common to two; we find them connected by reaves, and placed outside as well as inside the pounds; two-chambered huts are also found, and in no other settlements are there huts with entrances in a more complete state. The division of the pound into a number of spaces is also an arrangement seldom met with, and such a number of these enclosures in close proximity will not be seen in any other part of Dartmoor. From Huntingdon to Shipley, a distance of not quite three miles, fully a score of pounds are met with. Brent is the best case for the investigation of the remains in the valley of the Avon, which, as already observed, include not only those that have come down to us from a very early time, but also much that belongs to a later period. One particularly interesting relic of old Dartmoor is to be seen at Hickaton. This is the Abbots' Way, a path used by the monks of Buckfast and Buckland. It crosses the Brock Hill stream, and shortly after runs through one of the ancient pounds we have been noticing, the wall of which has been broken down to admit of its passing.

But we have reached the Wella Brook, and while pausing for a few brief moments to listen to its song we again see the shadowy horsemen as they come down to the ford. They ride at a rapid pace, and it is evident from their gestures that they have heard some news of the animals of which they are in search. We follow them, and passing up by the Avon, mount the hill of Western Whitabarrow, and crossing its shoulder descend towards the Erme. Idwallo looks down the valley where the river hides itself between folding banks, and seems to ask a question. But Modred shakes his head, and points to a ridge that lies before them. They urge forward their steeds, and speedily gain its summit. For a moment their forms are seen against the sky, and then they disappear, and when we reach the spot they are far down the slope that stretches to the Plym.

In this part of the valley through which that river runs there are several pounds. One of these is to be seen very near to Plym steps, on the left bank of the river, and another on the slope of Hart Tor, on the right bank. Near a small lateral valley, called Deadman's Bottom, which branches from Langcombe Bottom, there is also a pound. To the first of these a story attaches that is found in at least two other places on the Moor, as well as in many other localities. It tells how this part of Dartmoor was once in the Forest, but was claimed by the parish of Shaugh in consequence of the parishioners having brought for burial in their churchyard the corpse of a man discovered in the valley, and which the parishioners of Lydford had refused to do, notwithstanding that the Forest was within their boundaries. This story, like the others, is an invention, of course, but it is nevertheless certain that a considerable tract of ground once in the Forest is now regarded as belonging to the parish of Shaugh.

Modred and Idwallo come from the pound by the tor. Again they urge their horses forward, and we follow them as they pass over the hill to the Swincombe valley. Avoiding the great mire at its head, they make their way below the piles of Fox Tor, and soon find themselves among a number of scattered huts. Further down there is a pound on the right, which the farmer has since turned into a newtake, and here, at the entrance to one of the huts, a man is standing. As soon as he perceives the horsemen he holds up his hand, and as Modred and his comrade ride towards him he waves it in a certain direction, for he has guessed what brings them to the valley. They look, and see their missing beasts grazing quietly in a corner of the enclosure.

Modred and Idwallo, after a brief rest, take leave of the man who has proved himself their friend, but the beasts are to be left awhile in his charge, for the owners do not design to return to the valley of the Avon until the morrow. They pass down to the Dart, and fording it, make their way up towards old Bellaford, and then descend to the sister stream that comes down from the lonely fen land lying beyond the ridge that lifts itself to the northern sky. The day is waning, and as they move across the wide waste the shadows are creeping up the tors, where crests are yet steeped in rosy light. And upward, slowly upward, until one after another the gilded pinnacles become dark, and when the horsemen climb the ridge beyond the Webburn, and Grim's Pound comes in sight, the smiles of the summer day are gone.

As we stand beside the rampart in the deepening gloom a party of men come down from Hameldon. It is the hunters returning from the chase, and no sooner are they perceived than many go forth to meet them. Two of their horses are laden with the beasts they have slain, which tusk and antlers proclaim to be the boar and red deer. They pass within the walls of their settlement, where Modred and Idwallo, who have come to claim the hospitality of their brethren, await them. Then the gloom grows deeper still; it becomes dark, and all is hidden from us. Mingled with the faint cry of the distant stream is the sighing of the night wind, and this alone strikes on our ear. No sound comes from within the rampart; all is silence there, and when the crescent moon shows herself above the bold scarp that shuts in the combe on one side, and becomes for us a lamp, we know how this should be. We look only upon the broken walls, and the roofless dwellings of a forgotten day; a place that knows man no more

It is night, and our wanderings must cease. But with the dawn we will be on the Moor again, for there is yet much for us to see.

* * *

6
Resting Places of the Men of the Hills

Eastern Whitabarrow

Scarcely has the old Moor awakened from his sleep to welcome the coming of the new day, when we again find ourselves where Walla and the Avon meet. Their place of union is fair to look upon; and not only has Nature ordered that this should be so, but she has also willed that their onward way should lie amid scenes of pleasantness. And so Avon and his sweet companion go singing to the sea, by wood, and field, and orchard, and only lose their happy smiles from the stream up the side of the hill to the south, in the footsteps of the good knights, who in the time of the third Henry perambulated the bounds of the Royal Forest. On the summit is an object which they refer to by name in their return to the writ of the King, and which then formed one of the bond-marks. This is a grave where sleeps one, or perchance more, of Dartmoor's early children; a huge cairn known as Eastern

Whitaburrow, and which you shall see from many a point in this southern part of the Moor.

Of all the objects of prehistoric antiquity on Dartmoor, other than pounds and dwellings, none have provoked less curiosity than the cairn, and for the reason that its object is evident. From the very earliest times men have raised piles of stones, or mounds of earth, over their dead. When Achan was put to death by the children of Israel "they raised over him a great heap of stones," and Herodotus in describing the mode in which the Scythians buried their kings, states that the body was laid in a grave on a bed of leaves, and over this was heaped a great mound, all who were taking part in the work striving and vieing with each other to make it as large as possible. We learn from Plutarch that when Damaratus died in Alexander's camp he was given a magnificent funeral, and that a vast mound of earth, eighty cubits in height, was raised as a monument by the soldiers. The tumulus, whether of earth or stone, is indeed a monument, and when we find a very large one we shall probably not be far wrong in supposing it to have been raised over someone of more than ordinary importance.

Explorations conducted among British cairns and barrows reveal a number of modes of interment beneath them. Sometimes the body was laid on the ground, usually it would appear on its side, and the stones or earth heaped over it; in other instances burnt bones only have been found, either loose or placed in an urn; and in others the mound has covered one or more kistvaens. The cairns of Dartmoor have not yielded much to the searcher, though what many of them, opened in earlier days, or destroyed in more recent ones by the newtake wall builder, may have done, is, of course, not known. The practice of opening and rifling barrows is one that obtained at a very early period. The Anglo-Saxon poem of Beowulf speaks of the weapons and personal ornaments hidden beneath the grave mounds, and there are others that tell of such being rescued from their places of concealment. There are several instances of the opening of barrows in the 13th and 14th centuries; indeed, it is said that in 1324 a grant was made by Edward II for opening such ancient burial mounds in Devon. Many traditions are related on Dartmoor of the rifling of kistvaens, but in the majority of instances the despoiler meets with no better fortune than did Darius when he opened the sepulchre of Queen Nitocris of Babylon. In a district like Dartmoor, where loose stones abound in so many places, it is to be expected that the cairn, or heap of stones, will be found much more frequently than the barrow, or mound of earth. But there are several of the latter on the high ridge of Hameldon, and some of these were opened by the late Mr. C. Spence Bate. In the centre of one, which he found to be encircled with a low ridge of stones, was a little cairn, about three feet high, and a few feet from this was a small heap of burnt bones, which he was able to identify as being human. With these were some fragments of charcoal, and a fine flint flake. In another barrow Mr Spence Bate also found a small cairn, and at a short distance from it five large flat stones lying side by side. Under one of these were some burned human bones, a fragment of charcoal, and the bronze blade of a dagger, and also the amber pommel inlaid with small gold pins. On Parnell's Hill, immediately above the remains on the Harbourne, which we have already noticed, are two cairns, 23 yards distant from each other, one being 78 yards in circumference, and the other 73 yards. Not far from this is another, less than half the size, and this Mr Spence Bate and I opened in 1889. It was the last time he was ever on the Moor. We got nothing from the cairn, but we passed several pleasant hours together on the Moor, and did not feel that our ramble was without its reward.

No object connected with ancient sepulture on Dartmoor furnishes so many examples as the cairn, and none so few as the dolmen, or cromlech. The latter term is the one generally used, but most antiquaries have discarded it for the former, the word being derived from "daul" a table, and "maen," stone, which, as the object may be said to bear a rude resemblance to a huge table, not incorrectly describes it. The term cromlech, on the other hand is derived from "crom," a circle, and "lech," a stone, and thus would seem to be more applicable to a stone circle than to the object in question. A dolmen consists of one very large stone raised upon others set upright in the ground, this capstone, or quoit, as it is often termed, being of considerable weight, and usually approaching a flattish, oval form. The supporters are generally three in number, though there are many instances in which these are more, but in the Dartmoor examples, so far as can be learnt from an examination of the few existing remains, three were not exceeded. As the kist has often been found in the barrow or cairn, so it has been supposed that the dolmen was once hidden beneath a tumulus. That such was often the case it is, however, impossible to believe. In the first place it is inconceivable that a monument so striking as some of the largest dolmens are, and which must have been raised with infinite trouble, would have been concealed from sight by earth and stones; and in the second it is quite certain that many dolmens now standing would not be in existence if they had ever been so hidden. Those who had denuded them of their covering would hardly be so careful, except perhaps in rare instances, as to allow them to go untouched. The dolmen was raised over the interment, and was evidently intended to be a memorial of one whom it was desired particularly to honour; it is therefore not reasonable to suppose that earth and stone were heaped over it so that no man might see it. I am quite aware that it is now thought by some antiquaries that the dolmens were raised by a race of people altogether distinct from those who erected the other monuments that have come down to us. Others, again find it difficult to regard such speculations seriously; almost as difficult, in fact, as to predict what new theories shall have superseded them by the time the world has made a few more journeys round the sun. But into this question it is not my province to enter; my purpose is simply to notice the state of the few dolmens in the Dartmoor country.

Eastern Whitaburrow measures 90 yards in circumference at its base, and 12 yards form base to summit. Here there is a slight depression, and in places the decaying moss has formed a very thin layer of soil. The birds of the air have dropped seeds into this giant cup, and a few plants have found a home there. I remember when some thirty years ago a wild raspberry flourished on this lofty spot. Upon the sides of the cairn the winds beat with fury when the storm king was abroad, but in the hollow the plant was well sheltered, and so that it raised not its head above the stone surrounding it the blast was unable to do it serious hurt. On the same hill, but further to the west is Western Whitaburrow, also a bond mark of the Forest. Here, about three hundred and fifty years ago, Sir William Petre, to whom the manor of South Brent had been granted set up a cross to mark the limits of the lands over which he possessed rights, and which extended to the confines of the Forest. Nearly three centuries later some vandals threw it down, and knocking off the arms, used the shaft as a chimney-breast in a small house that they erected on the cairn. This was about 1847, as I gathered many years ago from some of the men who helped to build the house, and who found shelter in it afterwards. These were peat-cutters who worked on some peat-beds near by; their homes were at Brent, and this being too far distant for them to go to and fro daily to their labour, they remained at Western Whitaburrow, or Petre's Cross as it was then, and is still, called, from the Monday until the following Saturday. I could never learn from them that anything was discovered in the cairn when they took the stones from it for their house. Many years ago I found the broken shaft of Petre's Cross among the fragments of granite and set it up. It was afterwards thrown down, but is now again erect. Western Whitaburrow is 63 yards in circumference.

At Ball Gate, where the road across Aish Ridge and Coryndon Ball reaches Brent Moor, is a fallen dolmen and a large despoiled cairn. The stones of the latter have no doubt gone to build the walls of the enclosure near by, but none of the former have been removed. Only one of the supporters now stands erect, but it should not be a matter of great difficulty to re-erect the dolmen, as it is but a small one. Inside the enclosures belonging to Treeland, which are close at hand, are hut circles, and these also occur on Coryndon Ball. Quite near are other remains which we shall notice when we come to speak of the stone rows on the Moor.

In this locality is the hill known as Three Barrows, or Three Burrows, from the fine cairns by which it is crowned, one of which is a particularly large size. It is here that we shall observe the reave referred to in our fourth article. It starts at the head of the East Glaze, and is carried up the hill for nearly a mile, and down the further side towards the Erme for a short distance. It runs into the cairns, which stand in a line, in precisely the same manner as the Chittaford reave runs into Lower White Tor. If it was ever a road it must of course have been constructed previously to the building of the cairns, unless, as in the case of White Tor, we are to believe that in the early days piles twenty or thirty feet high were not regarded as stumbling-blocks; but if this was not the case what are we to think of the cairn builders who so unkindly placed their huge heaps of stone upon a roadway, when there was ample room for their piles on either side of it and half a dozen more like them? On the side of the hill nearest to the Erme the reave has never been completed, and the lower layers of stones being in sight, it certainly does present the appearance of a track way, and this, it is probable, led to the idea that it was such being conceived. In 1557 this reave was a boundary, and probably had been for a very long time. It serves the same purpose now, and in my own opinion never served any other.

On the common near Shaugh, where there are a number of hut circles, is Hawks' Tor, and here a large stone, very similar in apperance to the capstone of a dolmen, may be seen occupying a curious position. One end of it rests upon the principal rock of the tor, which is only a very low pile and the other upon a rounded boulder, which in turn rests upon another part of the tor, of a lower level than the main one. The stone being suggestive of a dolmen has been claimed as such by some, but I do not incline to that belief myself.

Immediately within the gateway at Dunnabridge Pound is an object round which a great deal of interest has centred, on account of its having been regarded as the Lord Warden's Seat, once to be seen on Crockern Tor. But the report that it was brought from the tor is altogether incorrect, and has arisen in consequence of the pound having been confounded with the farm of the same name. At the latter there is a stone that more than 70 years ago was said to have been brought from the tor, when the seats and table of the stannators were despoiled in the latter part of the 18th century but nothing has ever been traced to the pound. The so-called Judge's Chair I believe to be a dolmen, and its situation in the wall of an ancient pound (I allude to the enclosure on the ruined vallum of which the present wall was erected) need not surprise us. In the Erme valley a kistvaen will be found occupying a very similar position in the wall of one of the pounds in Brown Heath. This dolmen was, perhaps, closed on all sides. At all events, there is a stone near it which would have served to form one side, and as this shows part of circular holes such as are known to have been made in the sides of closed dolmens, it is not unreasonable to suppose that such was its purpose.

On the border of Chagford Common was once a dolmen known as the Three Boys, but the vandal had laid it low, and carried away all the stones but one, so long ago as the time when Mr G. Waring Ormerod wrote his interesting antiquarian notices of the neighbourhood. In the parish of Drewsteignton is the well-known Spinsters' Rock, the only dolmen in Devonshire that is not on Dartmoor, and by far the finest example in the country.

* * *

7

The Narrow House of Death

Childe's Tomb

Often in some solitary part of the Moor, usually removed from the hut clusters, though not always so, the rambler will come upon a small oblong cavity in the ground, lined with slabs of granite, which from its form he will hardly fail to recognise as an ancient grave. These objects are known as kistvaens, a name which, though not indicative of their purpose, yet sufficiently describes them, for they resemble nothing so much as a stone chest, and this is the literal meaning of the word. It is pure Celtic, "cist" — the c having the sound of the English k — meaning a "chest," and "maen," "stone"; the v — Celtic f — is used as a mutation of m. Kistvaens vary in size, but most of the examples on Dartmoor are from about three to three and a half feet, and from two to two and a half feet wide. They consist of five flat stones, set on their edges, the longer ones forming the sides of the pit in which they are placed, and the two shorter its ends. The tops of these are level with the ground, and on them rested the fifth stone as a cover to the sarcophagus. There was no bottom stone, so that the interments rested on the soil. In very many instances the kist is surrounded by a small circle of stones, which were probably set round a low mound of earth, beneath which it was buried. Whether it was always so hidden cannot be determined from the Dartmoor examples, as in a large number of cases no trace of the covering material exists, but it seems reasonable to suppose that they were.

Very little has been discovered in the Dartmoor kistvaens to throw light upon the nature of the interments, for long before they became known to the antiquary the treasure-seeker had despoiled them, and thus it is that in every instance where the cover stone remains it is seen thrown on one side. But examinations of kistvaens in other places have revealed that which we cannot learn from those on the Moor. When the interment was that of a cremated body the ashes were either placed in the kist in a heap or in a cinerary urn; when it was by inhumation the body was laid in a contracted position. Ornaments, and the weapons of the deceased, were usually placed with the body, or with the ashes. It is not improbable that kistvaens will yet be discovered on Dartmoor, buried beneath some of the low tumuli, and these, having escaped the spoilator, may perhaps yield something of greater interest than has yet been found in them. At present little more than ashes and a few flints and fragments of pottery have rewarded the modern searcher.

Several of the Dartmoor kistvaens bear names, and most of these point to the belief of the peasantry that they are places in which treasure was once hidden. By the side of a green path in Tor Royal Newtake is a kist known as the Crock of Gold, and not very far from the summit of Yar Tor, on the Corndon side, is another called Money Pit. Near the edge of Fox Tor Mire is a kist called the Gold Box, and close to the corner of Pills Newtake is one which goes by the name of Money Box. Not very far from the head of the Langcombe Brook, a tributary to the Plym, is a kist which it has been sought to identify with an object mentioned by the Forest perambulators in 1240. Grymsgrove is named by them as one of the bond-marks, and there have been those who considered this had reference to the kist, and that it meant the grave of Grim. But there is much that is fanciful in this, for it does not appear that the Forest boundary line ever went to the kist. The jury who surveyed the bounds in 1609 certainly did not regard that object as being a bond-mark, for they not only drew their line about three-parts of a mile northward of it, but state their belief that the Grymsgrove of the old records was Erme Head. Further down Langcombe Bottom, and on the other side of the stream, that is to say, the southern, is another kistvaen, and there is also one near Calves Lake Tor, which is not far distant.

Among other places where kistvaens are to be seen may be mentioned Thrushel Combe, on the Plym; Wigford Down, between the Dewerstone and Cadaford Bridge; in Watern Newtake, near Princetown; on Lakehead Hill and near Bellaford Tor; in Roundy Park, near Post Bridge, and also between the Powder Mills and White Tor; one on Rippon Tor, and another on Forsland Ledge. Many years ago, when in search of Childe's Tomb, which at the time was little more than a heap of soil with one or two stones lying near it, I discovered that the calvary and cross, removed about 1812 by the builder of Fox Tor House, had been set up over a kistvaen. This was cleared out, and when the monument was re-erected some few years later the stones were placed so as to permit of the kist being seen. On the down near Hound Tor, in the parish of Manaton, a fine kistvaen formerly existed, but all that now remains of it is about half of the enclosing circle of slabs, and two of the stones of the kist, and such indeed has been its condition for a long time. In 1878 when on the spot I discovered who it was had wrought the damage. A road contractor at that time lived in the cottage at Swallerton Gate, which is near by, and the stones of the circle and the kist offering themselves as material well suited to his purpose, he had ruthlessly removed them and broken them up. The work of spoilation would have proceeded until not a vestige of the grave remained had it not chanced that someone who had heard of the kist came along, and desired to be taken to the spot. A gratuity was forthcoming, and this opened the road contractor's eyes. He perceived that the circle would be likely to prove of greater value to him if he left it alone than if broken up for road material, and so he stayed his hand. But he had already done sufficient to render the kistvaen a thing of little interest, though he was very careful to let those who came to see it discover that for themselves. From an ancient grandame, the mother of the road mender, or of his wife, I forget which — I gathered the story of the kist. We sat beside the peat fire, and she told how that a long, long time ago, there came a rich gentleman into the neighbourhood, and settled there. Nobody knew how he got his money, and nobody could tell how he spent it, while everybody was very certain that he never gave away any. But, nevertheless, all were agreed that he was very rich, and no doubt the men touched their caps to him, and the women curtseyed when they passed him, as was the approved custom in the days when the peasantry knew very little more than the cattle they tended. At length the rich gentleman died, and according to his wishes was buried on the common near Hound Tor, in the kist the road mender had so thoughtlessly nearly destroyed. "And what became of his money?" I asked. "That sir," replied the old lady, "was never found. All they could tell was that he was very, very rich." He may have been; but I should be inclined to think that his wealth had much of the character of the Humbert millions.

At the foot of Standon Down, and not very far from the farm of that name on the Tavy, is a kistvaen in a rather decayed state. In the neighbourhood there are other relics; among which is a cluster of hut circles, which sometimes go by the name of Stannon Houses. These are on the slope of the hill opposite to Ger Tor, which rises at the lower end of Tavy Cleave, and form one of three groups near the river. The other is on the western bank between Ger Tor and Cleave Tors, and also above the latter. Near them a reave, which from some points presents all the appearance of a stone row, may be seen carried along the side of the hill. Between these two clusters are the remains of mining operations on the banks of the Tavy, with some open workings, known as gerts, on the hillside. The third group of hut circles is situated on the slope of Watern Oke, very near to the head of the narrow defile in which the Cleave Tors rise. These huts, which are in a ruined state, are placed amid a small clatter, where the ground descends very steeply to the Tavy. Quite near the cluster the waters of this river are augmented by those of the Rattle Brook, and on the bank of this there are also hut circles. The little stream rises under Hunt Tor, and marks the limits of the Forest throughout its course.

Flowing roughly parallel to the Rattle Brook, and on the western side of the high ridge crowned by Great Links Tor, is the Lyd, a stream possessing considerable interest, both on account of the scenery it passes through, and from its associations. The narrow valley down which its upper waters run was early chosen by man as a suitable situation for his dwellings. The ruins of these may still be seen. There are two clusters: one below Arms Tor, and another under Noddon, and among the huts are some good examples. The Lyd rises between Woodcock Hill and Corn Ridge. On the summit of the latter is a cairn, and from this it is not unlikely that the height took its name. The Celtic form of "cairn" is "carn" from which word the transition would be easy. Similarly we may suppose that Corndon, in the neighbourhood of Dartmeet, obtained its name. Carn dun would be the hill of the cairn, or of cairns, and such the eminence in question truly is, there being several fine tumuli upon it. It is now usually called Corndon Down, but the last work is merely a duplication of the preceding syllable, of which many instances are found among the Moor people. Between Corn Ridge and the West Ockment is an object bearing a name which it has been supposed is also derived from a relic of the old days. The dolmen near Drewsteignton stands on a farm called Shilston, a name thought to be a corruption of shelf stone — "shil" being the Devon vernacular for "shelf" — and to be derived from the ancient monument. The capstone of the dolmen would represent the shelf, and the derivation is not an improbable one, though it is necessary to point out that an early form of the name of the farm is Silvestane. The object alluded to as exisiting under Corn Ridge is a tor bearing a name similar to that of this farm, one of two on the Moor so called, the other being near Throwleigh. The name of Shilstone Tor has thus been thought to indicate the former existence of a dolmen near it, but I am unable to arrive at such a conclusion myself. An overhanging rock, particularly if in a position more than ordinarily striking, would represent a shelf equally as well as the quoit of a dolmen would do.

On Thornworthy Down, in the vicinity of Chagford, is a kistvaen, discovered in 1879 by Mr Samuel Slade, on opening a little mound by the side of the tiny stream that falls into the South Teign, and which serves throughout the lower part of its course to mark the boundary line of the Forest. It is said that the kist, which the visitor will find to be an excellent example, contained a smaller one, which was removed. Some fragments of pottery, and a flint knife, with two or three other flints, were also discovered. The commons in the neighbourhood of Thornworthy are thickly scattered with the remains of Dartmoor's former people. By-and-by we will view them, but in passing shall merely notice the curious enclosure known as the Round Pound, and one or two other objects. This pound, which is situated close to the road where it runs by the field belonging to Batworthy, is small, but interesting from the arrangement of its walls. Its shape is roughly triangular, but within the outer vallum is another enclosure of a circular form, the space between the two being divided by low walls into six courts, in one of which is a hut circle. On the down near it are a large number of other hut circles and reaves.

The South Teign shortly before leaving the Moor flows between the homestall of Fernworthy and Loughten Hill. On the latter is a newtake belonging to the farm named, and in this is the small pile called Loughten Tor. Around this little tor are several hut circles, and one of them, not far from its summit, is perhaps as interesting an example of these ancient dwelligs as will be found on the Moor. It is of considerable size, being no less than thirty-two feet in diameter on the inside, and the wall is formed of very large stones indeed. But its peculiarity is a low bench of granite slabs running round the wall on the interior.

An interesting object may be seen northward of Lakeland Farm, which is situated on the head waters of the Bovey River. It is a circular pound fifty-six paces in diameter, but the wall is quite unlike that usually seen in similar enclosures on the Moor. Instead of the stones having been originally laid in courses; they are set on their edges in the ground. It is in an excellent state of preservation, and is valuable as exhibiting a style of building which, though never common on the Moor, there is yet evidence to show was once to be seen in places. One or two hut circles may be observed near the lower part of this interesting relic.

About a mile below where the Erme takes its rise it bends toward the south, and here above the left bank is a hill known as Brown Heath. Where this slopes towards a tributary stream bearing the name of Hook Lake are three large pounds. The northern one, which is close to Erme Pound, the enclosure once used at the time of the drifts, is very imperfect, but the other two are in a good state of preservation. The southernmost one of those is 338 yards in circumference, and the other, that is to say, the middle one of the three, is 426 yards. The wall of the latter is composed of very large stones, and in places it is yet nearly five feet high. In the centre of this pound is a hut circle, and another is placed near the entrance. Without the walls are the other hut circles, and a stone row, terminating in a kistvaen, set within a circle of upright stones, thirty feet in diameter. This is quite close to the wall of the pound, in fact the stones that formed a protection to the abodes of the living nearly touch the grey slabs that mark the resting-place of the dead.

Silence now reigns upon these long-deserted dwellings of the children of the Moor, but how different was it when old Cloten dwelt with his son in the hut in the great pound. Then the voice of the Erme often mingled with the shoutings of the men, and with the thunderings of the hoofs of cattle, driven in the morning to their pasturage, and evening to their shelter. But a day came when the Erme, as now, sang her song uninterrupted by other sounds. It was when the aged Cloten mourned his son, and his friends silently prepared the pyre. Let the ages roll back, and we will be silent spectators as he follows him to the narrow house of death.

8
Circles that Enshrine the Dust

The Langstone

In one of the dwellings that dot the slope outside the great pounds on Brown Heath a number of men are gathered watching the preparation of the morning meal. Pieces of flesh are being taken from a small circular cavity in the ground, in which also are a number of large pebbles. By means of these, heated in the fire that burns in the centre of the hut, the meat has been cooked. It is handed round as it is brought from the cavity; and the milk is also served in cups of coarse pottery, of a tall form, and ornamented with impressed straight and zigzag lines. The men, who use flint knives, eat their meal in silence, and it is evident that they are oppressed with sorrow. The skins that screen the doorway of the hut at night are drawn aside, and through the opening they look down upon the folding steeps between which the Erme glides snakelike on its way to the unseen oak woods that come up the valley to meet the wild moor. The heather had not yet purpled the slopes above the banks, but only tinged them with a dull red, as though Nature had refused to deck herself in her gay apparel in the sight of men whose hearts were filled with grief. When the meal is over, the occupants of the hut do not leave it, but sit moodily until the shadows cast upon the ground by near-by objects warn them that it is time to go forth. Then they pass out into the sunshine, and make their way to the entrance to the pound in which Cloten has fixed his abode. No cattle are seen within its wall of stone and turf, for scarcely was the new day born ere they were driven to a distant pasturage. And so all is silent, save the Erme, but her song is so low and sweet that it is hardly heard by those who gather at the gateway.

The body of Cloten's son is borne from the hut in the centre of the great enclosure. The old man follows, and behind him are weeping women and men and youths with downcast eyes. As they approach the gate of the pound the throng fall back, and when the mourners have passed, they follow them to the spot where the funeral pile is raised. This is of dry branches, and upon it are hung the spear and the bow of the departed. The body is laid upon it, and presently the wood fire is lighted. As the smoke ascends the sounds of lamentation rise also; and are wafted by the morning breeze through the solitary valley. When the body is consumed the ashes are gathered and placed in an earthen vessel, which is borne to the open kist near by, and there deposited, with an arrow and a flint axe and knife. Then the cover is placed on the kist, and stones are set up in a circle around it. It is close to the wall of the pound in which is Cloten's habitation, for the aged man desires that he may be ever near the ashes of his son.

Circles formed of upright stones belong to that class of monuments formerly known as Druidical, and were once supposed to be temples. When they enclose a kist or a cairn, we know, of course, that their purpose was sepulchral, but in many of the larger examples no such objects exist. But examinations of similar remains in other parts of the world, without which no satisfactory conclusion regarding them, or other megalithic monuments, could be arrived at, show that though kist or cairn may be absent the purpose of the circle was still to mark the resting-place of the dead. Thus, the principal stone circles on Dartmoor, such as those at Scorhill, Little Hound Tor, Langstone Moor, Stall Moor, and the Grey Wethers, have probably no more significance than the smaller ones that surround the numerous kistvaens. No religious idea is to be traced in either, though we cannot, of course, say they formed no part of the apparatus of Druidism, any more than did the logans, the tolmen in the Teign, or the rock basins on the tors. That priesthood existed on Dartmoor only is the fancy of those who wrote about the region in the earlier part of the 19th century. Leigh Hunt, speaking of Keats, said, "He never beheld an oak tree without seeing the Dryad"; so the antiquary of sixty or seventy years ago never looked upon a stone circle without seeing a Druid in the middle of it.

Crossing the Erme at the foot of Brown Heath, which, unless the stream is in flood we shall be able to do by means of the boulders in its channel, we mount the slope of Outer Stall Moor, and here we shall come upon a stone row. Following this in a southerly direction we shall be led for a considerable distance, and shall find as we advance that the stones composing the row gradually increase in size. It terminates in a fine stone circle, which, though not so large as some to be found on the Moor, is in a very good state of preservation. Being at a considerable distance from any enclosures it has escaped the spoilator, while Time has been particularly kind, having laid its hand only upon three of the twnety-six stones of which the circle consists. These are of an average height of two and a half feet, but there is one double that height. The diameter of the circle is fifty-four feet. But what renders this monument particularly interesting is the stone row connected with it, and which, as we have just seen, runs for a long distance over the heath. It terminates in a dilapidated kistvaen on the summit of Green Hill, within the Forest, and can be plainly traced nearly the whole of the way. The principal break in it is on the side of the hill named, but it is met with again higher up, where it is seen crossing Middle Mires. About half a mile from the circle the row crosses a shallow hollow, through which a rivulet courses to the Erme, and near this is a mossy cairn, forty-four yards in circumference, but only a few feet in height. In this hollow are the remains of tin streaming operations, and it is interesting to note that the stone row is carried through these. It is to be seen not only on the sides of the little combe, but also on the uneven ground in the bottom of it, where the tinners worked. Mr C. Spence Bate noticed this circle and row in a paper read before the members of the Devonshire Association in 1871, and I also briefly described them in the second volume of the "Antiquary," 1880. Nine years later they were "discovered" by the writer of a book on the Moor, who expressed surprise that these objects had not been noticed by anyone.

Not very far from the Stall Moor Circle, and between it and the Erme, is a pound containing hut circles; but in a very decayed state. The enclosure is divided into several parts by low walls in a similar manner to those we have noticed elsewhere. On Erme Plains, on the other side of the river, are also a number of hut circles; in fact, relics of an olden day line the banks of the stream from a point just below Red Lake Foot to Harford Bridge. This part of the Erme Valley is readily reached either from Ivybridge or Cornwood. If the rambler proceeds from the former, he may, by passing up the hill to the Moor gate above Stowford, find himself in the midst of numerous remains soon after entering on the common. On the slope above Addicombe, near Lukesland, are a few decayed hut circles and a small irregularly shaped pound. A little further up, and about midway between Addicombe and Butterdon Hill, is another pound, 165 yards in circumference, divided into two parts by a wall running across it. In the south-west corner is a hut circle, close to the wall, and outside the latter is another, also joined to it. On the south-east are two more, without the wall, like the others, touching it. The vallum of this enclosure is very much overgrown. On the summit of Butterdon Hill are three cairns, the largest of which measures 92 yards in circumference; another is 80 yards, and the third 50 yards, and near them are other remains. On the north-west slope of the hill there is also a cairn, 53 yards in circumference, and many others may be seen on the neighbouring heights. Indeed, that part of Dartmoor lying between the Erme and the Glaze, and which comprises the southern portions of Ugborough and Harford Moors, might well be styled the land of cairns. Tumuli are found on Ugborough Beacon, and on the ridge stretching from it northward; on the Western Beacon above Ivybridge, where there are no less than six, one of them being 85 yards in circumference; on Butterdon Hill, as we have just seen; on Weatherdon Hill, where there are two fine ones; on Sharp Tor, above Piles Newtake; on the wind-swept height of Three Barrows, and in other places.

The rambler up the valley of the Erme will find many good examples of hut circles between Addicombe and Harford Moor Gate and whether he crosses the stream at Harford Bridge and passes upwards above its right bank, or continues on his way by Piles and Erme Plains to Brown Heath, he will be surrounded during his progress by similar objects, as well as by other remains of a most interesting character. Between Harford Bridge and Outer Stall Moor, on the right bank of the Erme, are three fine stone rows, one being that which we have already seen starting from the circle, besides several enclosures, and the cairn crowning the hill known as Stalldon Barrow. On the left, or eastern bank, there is the kistvaen at the corner of Piles Newtake; many curious hut circles within the newtake; some large examples of these ruined dwellings on Erme Plains; and the enclosures we have already noticed on Brown Heath, and which are usually known as Erme Pound Rings.

A story is related of the circle on Stall Moor, which object sometimes goes by the name of the Dancers, and also as Kiss-in-the-Ring. A number of lasses — but of what village I cannot tell you — set off one Sunday afternoon for the Moor, and on finding themselves out of sight of the farmhouses, quite forgot what day it was, and began to indulge in a dance. By-and-by a young countryman came by, and a unanimous wish was expressed that he should join them. He consented on condition that kiss-in-the-ring was substitued for the dance. the proposal was received with acclamation, and the lasses having formed a ring the youth set out on his march around it. But the ordinary conditions of the game were soon disregarded by the damsels. One youth among so many meant that they could only be kissed very seldom, and this did not at all suit their wishes. As, therefore, the young man in spite of his endeavours failed to please them, since he could only kiss one at a time, they soon fell to kissing him, and half a dozen pairs of rosy lips were pressed against his cheeks at once. At first he rather enjoyed it, but by-and-by the truth of the adage that it is possible to have too much of a good thing was brought home to him. He broke and fled. But the maidens were not disposed to allow one upon whom they had showered their favours, and whose company they still desired, to escape them, and so they set off, one after the other, in pursuit. The foremost damsel had nearly reached the fugitive when a weird and wonderful thing happened. Instantly the maidens were turned to stone, and there they still stand in a long line, a warning to those who shall indulge in kiss-in-the-ring on Sundays, or, it may be, who fail to observe the rules of the game.

The western side of Stall Moor is bounded by the River Yealm, and on the left bank of this, and at no great distance from its source, are two pounds, placed close together, one being much larger than the other. That part of the wall common to both is much smaller than the part forming the outer defence, which if taken as being one main vallum measures 635 yards in circumference. The stones composing it are not very large, but it is perfect throughout. On the south-south-west is an entrance to the pound, on each side of which stands a large slab, placed at right angles to the wall, and about four feet in height. On the other side of the enclosure, and nearly opposite to this, is what appears to have been another entrance. In the largest, or eastern, division there are sixteen hut circles, some of them being in a very good state of preservation; in the smaller division there are five of these ancient dwellings. Outside the wall there are many others, there being more than a dozen on the slope to the south of the pounds, and some to the north of it. It is here where the finest examples of hut circles with very wide walls, to which allusion has been made, are to be seen. One of a group of five, forty-five yards to the north of the pound, has a wall of stone and turf no less than ten feet thick. Thirty yards from the pound in a south-easterly direction is a kistvaen enclosed within a small circle thirteen feet in diameter, but the turf has encroached upon it to such an extent that it is hardly distinguishable.

These fine hut enclosures, which are generally known as Yealm Head Rings, are not very far above Hawns and Dendles, and are easily reached from Cornwood. The Moor is entered by the gate near Watercombe Farm, from which point a track runs up past the Rings, which are about a mile and a half distant. Midway another large pound is passed on the left, and in this there are also a large number of hut circles. On the banks of the Yealm, quite close to which these hut clusters are, the evidences of the presence of the tinners are everywhere observable.

Among the other stone circles on Dartmoor is one on Langstone Moor, in the parish of Petertavy, which we find spoken of as having been "discovered" in 1894, by which we presume it is meant that attention was first directed to it in that year. At that time the whole of the stones were down, but they have since been re-erected. Its diameter is about fifty-six feet. Whether there was ever a second circle outside this one, as has been supposed, is open to question, but if such were the case it would not be the only instance on the Moor of a circle within a circle. In 1878 I found one on the common not far from Ephraim's Pinch, but so much overgrown with furze that it was difficult to obtain a correct measurement of it. However, I found the outer circle to be forty-five feet in diameter, and to be formed of slabs similar to those in another small circle in the neighbourhood, which stands on Soussons Common, not far from Runnage Bridge; the diameter of the inner circle was about twenty feet. What must have been a very fine circle once stood on the slope of Down Ridge, in the vicinity of Hexworthy, but only a very few stones now remain; and another partially destroyed is to be seen on Sherberton Farm. Near Siddaford Tor are the two circles known as the Grey Wethers. These are quite close to each other, and had they not been injured, probably by newtake wall builders, would form a fine monument. There are others that can be more conveniently mentioned when we speak of the stone rows.

That within the stone circles of Dartmoor is enshrined the dust of many of her hardy children we cannot doubt. But that only do we know. The stones may also have had some mystic meaning, and that we can never discover. When Joshua commanded the twelve men from the tribes to take each a stone from Jordan, they were told that they were to do this that it mightt be a sign among them, and among their children. But of the monuments raised by the early men of Dartmoor our only knowledge is that they mark the spots where the dead were laid, and we have no further answer should we be asked "What mean these stones?"

* * *

9

The Way of the Sepulchre

The Cemetery

Southward of the hill of Three Burrows rise the two branches of the Glaze, an affluent of the Avon, and falling into that river about a mile below the little market town of South Brent. The confluence of these branches, named respectively the East and West Glaze, is in a delightful valley formed by the ridge northward of Ugborough Beacon on one side, and by the tree-covered steep known as Coryndon Wood on the other. This valley takes its name from the stream, but it is seldom heard in the neighbourhood, the natives preferring to substitute Glascombe Bottom for the true appellation of Glaze Combe. On the common a few score yards westward of Glaze Meet, as the confluence is always called, but high above the stream, is a fine pound, the situation of which is hardly less pleasing than that of Gripper's Pound, on the Avon, while the enclosure itself is infinitely more striking in appearance. The wall, as in other examples, is in ruins, but with the exception of a few openings made to allow of tracks being carried through the pound has apparently been untouched. The fallen stones cover a space of about ten feet across where it is at its widest, but its height is not great. Growing in the wall are several moss-covered thorn bushes and a holly, and ferns also find a home in the interstices of the granite blocks of which it is composed. In the pound are two decayed hut circles, and springing from the wall of one of these is another thorn, which, with its fellows, flourishes in spite of the storms of winter, putting forth bud and leaf in season. This growth gives the enclosure a more picturesque appearance than that usually worn by the walled settlements on the Moor. Its circumference is 422 yards.

But let us make our way thither, for near it are other objects for us to see. As we approach we discover that the pound is not without occupants. By the doorway of one of the dwellings is Natan, seated on the ground and engaged with an assistant in chipping a flint, a work in which he has gained much proficiency, while Gerwin is standing by and watching the proceeding with curiosity. Natan holds the flint flake in his left hand, where it rests on the palm, and is kept in position by the fingers. In his right hand he has a small tool, also of flint, and this he places on those parts of the flake he desires to break off, while his assistant strikes it with a mallet. The work has been in progress for some little time, and the flake is now assuming the required shape. When one side of it is chipped Natan turns it, and the other side is similarly treated. This is repeated several times, until at length the work is finished, and he holds up an arrow-head with an expression of satisfaction. Gerwin turns away, and quitting the pound goes towards the river, where a number of men are gathering. We will leave Natan and his flints, and follow him.

At the head of a wooded hollow where the bare commons rise on either side of the Glaze, the banks of the stream have been much disturbed. Stripped of their covering of turf, only dark soil and stones are seen, many of the latter being thrown up in heaps. When Gerwin reaches the spot he sets to work with his fellows, and presently the bright waters are dulled by the earth and sand that falls into them as more stones are loosened, and roughly piled on their margin. From among them a number of dark lumps are picked out and placed on one side. Presently men come and carry them away to be crushed. The rude mortar is not far off. It is simply a block of granite, and on this the lumps are broken up with pounding stones. When the work is done the gravel is washed, and one part of it is separated from the other. This is the tin ore, and by-and-bye it will be carried to the pound, there to remain until strangers by whom it is valued shall come and offer something in exchange for it.

Near the head of the working we leave it, and turn towards the East Glaze. About midway between the two streams we shall come upon a group of stones placed in rows, and forming one of those monuments found in so many places on the Moor, and which have been the subject of so much speculation. This group, which was first described by Mr C. Spence Bate, has been referred to as being on Coryndon Ball, which, however, is incorrect. It is situated on The Glazes, a piece of common taking its name from its situation between the branches of the streams so-called, and which in a list of waste lands in the vicinity, of the date 1812, is set down as containing 64 acres 1 rood and 15 perches. The group is interesting only on account of the number of the parallel lines of stones; beyond this it possesses no importance. The stones themselves are small, many of them indeed being level with the turf, and the remains are so insignificant that they might easily be passed without attracting notice. The rows are eight in number, or, perhaps it may be more correct to say, there are seven in one group and an eighth running parallel to these a few yards distant, but forming another monument. The seven start from a circle, only a few stones of which now remain, while the single row is connected with a dilapidated cairn. The first extend westward for a distance of about eighty yards, but the latter is rather longer. Rather over a quarter of a mile in an easterly direction is the fallen dolmen and despoiled cairn at Coryndon Ball Gate, which we have already noticed. There does not appear to be any connection between these monuments, nor is there any reason for supposing such to have been the case.

Stone rows are found in different parts of England, as well as in Scotland and other countries, but nowhere are they so numerous as on Dartmoor. Many suggestions have been made respecting their purpose, but that they are purely sepulchral is the only conclusion at which it is possible to arrive after an examination, and a study of them in the light of modern antiquarian discovery. As Lord Avebury had observed, all stone monuments may be considered as parts of one common plan; some may have been memorials or temples, but the idea is still that of an interment. The Dartmoor rows are sometimes a single line of stones, sometimes a double line, and a few exceed this, as in the instance just noticed. That the number of the rows in a monument had a special meaning is very probable. The monument itself being of an important character, and one not frequently met with, we may well suppose to have been erected as a memorial of some chief or headman, the rows branching from the place of his interment. The stones composing the row may have represented his followers, or those with whom he was in some way intimately associated. Two rows may have been set up when the latter belonged to two different settlements, or, which is more likely, the second was added when another interment of some member of the headman's family took place. Further interments might in some cases call for similar memorials, and other rows would be added, until a monument such as that on The Glazes would be formed. But to pursue this is only to enter upon unprofitable speculations. All that we can be sure of is that the rows are sepulchral; that these long lines of stones were set up as memorials of those who repose in some near by kist or cairn; that they pointed the way to the tomb.

On the slope of the hill, and westward of the great stream work in Glaze Combe, is another row, which is peculiarly interesting, one portion of it consisting of a single line of stones, and the other of a double line. On the brow of the ridge, but further to the south, is a single row starting from a small cairn, another cairn also being near it. I called the attention of the late Mr R. N. Worth to this row when he was preparing a paper on these monuments some years ago, but he evidently supposed that I was referring to the former row, for he describes that while giving the situation of this one. We are here again on Ugborough Moor, where, as already stated, cairns are numerous. One of these is built round the westernmost pile of Ugborough Beacon, and a short distance from it in a south-westerly direction is another. Further on in the same direction are two more, one being 94 yards in circumference and the other 70 yards. Northward of the Beacon are many others, among which may be mentioned one bearing the name of Glas Barrow.

Passing over the common towards the south-west we reach Butterdon Hill, previously noticed, and here we shall find a circle thirty-five feet in diameter, enclosing a small cairn. The whole of the stones have fallen, but the circle is nevertheless not without interest, as a very long stone row starts from it. The row runs northward from this crumbling relic, and like the reave on the side of the hill of Three Barrows, has for long formed a parish boundary. It serves as a line of demarcation to Ugborough and Harford Moors, and may be traced for a distance of 1,791 yards. The stones composing it are placed at an average distance of three and a half feet apart, and are rather less than a foot and a half in height. There are however, some larger ones. One, which is fallen, measures five and a half feet in length, and another four and a half feet. the boundary of the two Moors named is marked beyond the termination of the row by ordinary bond stones, which may be seen on Erme Plains and on Brown Heath, beyond Hook Lane.

We have referred to three rows on the western side of the Erme, one being that running from the circle on Stall Moor. Another is on Burford Down, near Harford Bridge, and a third on the western shoulder of the hill crowned with Stalldon Barrow. The latter consists of fine stones, most of which Time has dealt hardly with. These are all single rows, but further up the stream there is a double one. This will be found between the two pounds on Brown Heath, running up from the lower one to the circle enclosing the kistvaen, in which we have supposed the son of Cloten to be laid.

On lands belonging to Cholwich Town Farm is a stone row, and others are to be seen at Trowlesworthy Warren, on the Plym, each connected with a circle. Further up the stream named, at Thrushel Combe, locally Drizzlecombe, are three rows with menhirs and other important remains, and near Down Tor, on the Newleycombe Lake is another. Both these latter groups may be conveniently reached by the pedestrian from Princetown, a centre from which many interesting remains may be visited. Below Hart Tor, and only about a mile and a half from the village, are two rows, one double, and the other single. They both start from cairns, the one at which the double row has its commencement being surrounded by a stone circle. Near by are hut circles, and these also occur on Raddick Hill, which is not far off, and at other places in the immediate vicinity. In a hut circle on the hill named Mr Robert Burnard found, in 1896, a cooking-pot of coarse hand-made pottery; and pieces of pottery were also discovered in Yes Tor Bottom near the Princetown railway. Beyond Raddick Hill are several huts on Roundy Farm, below Crazy Well Pool, and among them is a small enclosure of a very curious character. From Princetown also the well-known remains near Merrivale Bridge are easily reached. These consist of a circle, two double rows, and a fine menhir, besides other remains. Hut circles are numerous, and among them are some good examples.

On the common on the east side of Cosdon is a monument known in the locality as The Cemetery, consisting of three rows of stones, starting from a double kist. Until a few years ago it was in a very ruinous condition, but a careful restoration has given it something of its old time appearnce on the slopes. Below this rude burial place are huts, though not so many as formerly, for much land has been here reclaimed, and they have been destroyed; above it rises the huge hill of Cosdon, on the summit of which cairns mark another burial-place. A track, leading from South Zeal to the Forest, runs by this monument, and a short distance beyond Raybarrow Pool passes a stone circle, the positon of which renders it a very striking object. This has been restored, and for its preservation, as well as that of the Cemetery, we are indebted to the Rev. S. Baring-Gould. On the north side of the ridge on which it is placed, that is towards the Taw, is a group of hut circles with several reaves. These are situated on a tributary of that river called Small Brook, and are not without interest.

Among other stone rows on Dartmoor may be mentioned those at Assacombe and Waters Down, and also the one on Challacombe Down. The latter was first noticed by Mr John Prideaux in 1828. For many years the stones lay prone upon the ground, many being hidden by the heather. Now, however, they are once more erect, and the visitor to Grim's Pound may look across the valley and see them plainly marked against the sky.

* * *

10

The Pillar of Witness

Beardown Man

Of the various kinds of megalithic monuments it was probably the menhir that most frequently had a meaning apart from the sepulchral one. The form and arrangement of the others show them to have been receptacles of the dead, or structures raised over them. The dolmen is obviously only a huge kist; the kist itself is a rude coffin; the circle simply marks a place of burial, as is proved by its frequent occurrence round a kist or a cairn; and the stone row, though perhaps possessing a peculiar meaning, is still but a part of each of these, and indeed not improbably originated in an extension of the passage leading to the centre of the chambered tumuli. But there is nothing of a sepulchral character in the appearance of the menhir, and though we know that in most instances it was connected with interments, we have also evidence that it was sometimes set up to commemorate events. When Jacob rose up early in the morning in the place that he called Bethel, he "took the stone that he had put for his pillow, and set it up for a pillar," and, having vowed a vow, he said, "And this stone, which I have set up for a pillar, shall be God's house." Again, when the patriarch was overtaken by Laban in the Mount of Gilead, and they had made a covenant, "Jacob took a stone and set it up for a pillar," and his brethren also took stones and made a heap. "And Laban said to Jacob . . . This heap be witness, and this pillar be witness, that I will not pass over this heap to thee, and that thou shalt not pass over this heap and this pillar unto me, for harm." When God appeared unto Jacob, when he came out of Padan-aram, and gave the land to him and to his seed, "Jacob set up a pillar in the place where he had talked with Him, even a pillar of stone." And again, when Rachel died, and was buried in the way to Ephrath, "Jacob set up a pillar upon her grave." We find also that Absalom reared a pillar for himself in the King's dale, "for he said, I have no son to keep my name in remembrance: and he called the pillar after his own name." While the unwrought obelisks to be found on Dartmoor appear to be all connected with interments, in the light of the foregoing we may not unreasonably conclude that some, at least, were also intended to be commemorative of an important event.

The name by which the Dartmoor native calls these rude pillars is the same as that by which they are known to the archæologist, only the latter uses the Celtic form while the former is content with the English. They are popularly known as longstones, not only on the Moor, but in most places in England, and this is precisely the meaning of the word menhir, which is simply the Celtic maen (stone) and hir (long). Of unhewn granite the appearance of the Dartmoor examples is rude in the extreme, and in consequence of their usually wild surroundings is to a certain extent impressive. Their height varies; that of the Longstone on Dean Moor is eight feet, the well-known menhir on Long Ash Hill, near Merivale, is between ten and eleven feet, and the one in the vicinity of Kes Tor is about ten feet. But the finest is the menhir at Thrushel Combe, which when lying on the ground before its re-erection measured very nearly eighteen feet in length.

In the parishes around the Moor several inscribed stones have been found, but these are of later date than the unwrought pillars, and belong to an altogether different class of monuments. Among these may be named the three stones preserved in the vicarage garden at Tavistock, one of which was obtained in the immediate neighbourhood, and the other two in the parish of Buckland Monachorum; and the stone formerly existing at Fardel, near Cornwood, which is now in the British Museum. These are of the Romano-British period, and do not come within the compass of our remarks. One monument, however, of historic times must be mentioned, as it was probably fashioned out of a menhir. It is the cross by the side of the Okehampton road, where it passes over Sourton Down, now enclosed. The shortness of the arms, which project only about two and a half inches, certainly seems to point to this Christian monument having been formed out of a rude pagan monolith. It bears an inscription which the Rev. S. Baring-Gould, who was the first to decipher it, considers to belong to the sixth century.

The menhir referred to as being situated near Kes Tor stands in the midst of a most extensive group of remains, consisting of circles, stone rows, pounds and huts. Close to the ground this monolith is nine feet in girth, but diminishes in size upward, its top being of a wedge shape. It serves as a bond mark of the Forest, and also of the commons belonging to Gidleigh and Chagford, the initial letters of the names of those two parishes, and also of Dartmoor, being cut upon it. A double stone row runs from the menhir in a northerly direction, and at its termination another row of the same character starts from a decayed cairn; near where the latter ends two other rows also double are to be seen. From these two rows the ground slopes towards the North Teign, on the further side of which, and not far from the confluence of that stream and the Walla Brook, is the fine Scorhill Circle. This is a good example of this class of monument, notwithstanding that it has suffered at the hands of the despoiler. It is not so very long since that one of the stones was split, apparently to form gateposts, but attention being drawn to the matter its removal was prevented. Representations having been made in the proper quarter, it is to be hoped that the circle will suffer no further damage. In this part of the Moor, on and near Buttern Hill, are the remains of two other fine circles, and the one already referred to as being situated near Little Hound Tor is also at no great distance to the north. Very near to the latter is Whitemoor Stone, which, like the Longstone just noticed, acts as a bond mark of the Forest, and of two commons — those belonging to the parishes of Gidleigh and Throwleigh. The stone is not very high, but there seems to be no reason for not regarding it as a genuine menhir. Not only does its proximity to the circle show this,. but it is altogether different in character from an ordinary bondstone.

From the Longstone near Kes Tor a double row of stones formerly extended in a southerly direction to the dolmen, once to be seen here, called the Three Boys, and to which reference has already been made. The rows have, however, entirely disappeared, the stones having been removed by those who built the Thornworthy Newtake walls near by. About a mile from the Longstone is the farmhouse of Fernworthy, and not far from this, on Froggymead Hill, is a circle a little over sixty feet in diameter. The stones comprising it are not very large, but with the exception of two or three they retain their original position. Connected with this circle are some stone rows, first noticed by the late Mr George Wareing Ormerod in 1858, and on Long Ridge, to the west of it, is a group of hut circles.

On the slope of Lough Tor, and not very far from the well-known Bellaford Tor, is a fallen menhir, and in connection with it are the remains of a double stone row. Northward of Bellaford Tor is Lakehead Hill, on which are pounds, one of them bearing the name of Krapp's Ring, and also some kistvaens. In this neighbourhood there are a number of enclosures, some very ancient, and it is not unlikely that more than one monument was destroyed by those who built the walls. But notwithstanding that such may have been the case, much that is interesting is still to be seen. On either side of the East Dart are pounds with hut circles — one on Broad Down, about a mile above Post Bridge, being particularly noticeable.

We have already mentioned the pounds and cairns on Dean Moor. The latter are situated on Parnell's Hill, and a short distance off, in a direction east by south, is the menhir above spoken of. This is a slab three feet nine inches wide at the base, and one foot wide at the top. It is thirteen inches thick, and its height, as we have before stated, is eight feet. On the further side of the hill, to the north of the menhir, is the commencement of the long reave that runs up to the summit of Pupers, and beyond that hill is Snowdon, which extends to the Mardle. On the crest of Snowdon are four cairns placed in a line running north and south. The southernmost one is the largest, and measures eighty yards in circumference. The stones in this one, and in the next to it, are covered with short, grey moss. One the further side of the Mardle, towards the north-east, is a hill known to the Moormen as Nap, and on the summit of this there are also four cairns, one of them being very large. Like those on Snowdon, they are covered with vegetable growth, much of this, however, being turf, of which they appear to be partly formed.

Among the remains at Thrushel Combe are three menhirs, one being the large one already referred to. These, which were long prostrate on the turf, were re-erected in the summer of 1893, and with the rows and other objects form an exceedingly interesting group of antiquities. In the following year the menhirs on the common near Down Tor, about a mile and a half to the north of Thrushel Combe, were also set up. The ancient Abbots' Way, which runs from Marchants Bridge, near Meavy, by Ringmoor Cot, and to the north of Ringmoor Down, passes very near to the Thrushel Combe group of remains. Down Tor is reached from Dousland by way of Nosworthy Bridge.

One of the commons bordering upon the Forest seems to have derived its name from a menhir. This, which is situated in Peter Tavy parish, between the Walkham and Cudlipp Town Down, is known to the dwellers in the neighbourhood as Lanson Moor, a name which appears on the Ordnance map as Launceston Moor. But there is little doubt that Lanson is really a corruption of Langstone, and that the piece of common so called took its name from the fine obelisk on its western side, and which until a few years ago lay prostrate on the ground. In the vicinity of this are many objects that will detain the antiquary. On the summit of White Tor, which is close by, is the enclosure containing hut circles, to which allusion has been made as being the only one on Dartmoor occupying a site suitable for defence; on the eastern verge of the common is the stone circle already noticed, and which was re-erected a few years since by the Duke of Bedford, the Rev. S. Baring-Gould superintending the restoration; between it and the Walkham is a pound, with hut circles both within and without it; and there are also other groups of hut circles around the common.

In two instances the Celtic word maen is preserved in the name of the unwrought pillar. One of these is Bear Down Man, the great stone near the source of the Cowsic, on which the warrener Nicholas Edgecombe discovered the hairs of the Scotch bullocks, as readers of "The River," Eden Phillpott's delightful story, will remember. The other is Quintin's Man, which now exists only in name. It is borne by a cairn situated at a short distance from the head of the North Teign, but there can hardly be a doubt that on or near this a menhir was once to be seen. Its disappearance is easily to be accounted for, since the enclosures of Teign Head Farm are close by. It is rather curious to note that the name Quintin's Man is essentially the same as menhir, for one of the meanings of the word quintin, or quintain, is a post. It is derived from the French, and the name may have become attached to the monolith in Norman times, though I do not forget that Quintin as the name of an individual occurs more than once in Dartmoor history. In the neighbourhood the cairn is often called Quinter's Man, but this is merely a local form of the name.

In this brief survey of the prehistoric monuments of Dartmoor we have been able to do little more than glance at a few interesting groups, but such as we have here noticed may be taken as representative of the others. That certain conclusions at which I have arrived concerning them will not be shared by some is very likely, but I can only say that they have not been hastily reached. My investigations of the stone remains of our western highlands spread over a period of more than thirty years. I have had no theory regarding them that I wished to build up; I have sought only to learn their story. But the centuries have rendered all so dim that I found it difficult to grope my way, and what my search has yielded seems poor indeed. Still, the stones tell a story to me, and it is one they will tell to all if they only be listened to. We may be unable to deduce a religious idea from individual monuments; it may not be possible to bring forward a scrap of evidence to show that any of the circles were temples; we may admit, and shall probably be right in so doing, that they were altogether unconnected with any form of worship; but, notwithstanding this, those monuments most surely have some sort of a religious signification. If the stones of Dartmoor tell us anything, they tell us that the men who dwelt amid its ancient hills, and set up the menhir and the circle, and built the cairn, honoured those who had gone before. The position in which the body was placed in the kist, revealed by explorations elsewhere, and the weapons deposited with it, tell us, too, that those who laid their brother there believed that he yet lived in the spirit land. It was this that prompted them to raise the massive dolmen, and pile up the huge cairn.

Polwhele, the historian of Devon, looked upon Dartmoor as a home of Druidism — a belief intensely interesting, but unfortunately there is no evidence to support it. Yet it cannot be declared that it never found a place there. Cæsar tells us that it was the religion of the people of South Britain, and no one can say that it did not penetrate into the West. We know not how this may be; we neither affirm nor deny that the early men of Dartmoor had religious teachers. But we do hold that the columnar circle and the rude monolith proclaim that those who raised them had a belief in a life beyond the grave, as clearly as though their places were taken by the symbol of the Christian faith.

But the shadows warn us that the day is drawing to a close, and in the calm of the evening hour we set our faces towards the ingrounds where is home and rest. On the faint breeze is born the music of the little stream, the same sweet melody that was heard in the olden days by those who dwelt in the huts whose sites are marked by the ruins around us. Now the fickle wind wafts the sound from us, and it dies away until it becomes a whisper. It is a voice coming up out of the years long flown, for we feel that it spoke to the sons of the wilderness who reared the walls of yonder pound, and who now sleep beneath the mossy cairn that crowns the height beyond the stream. The forms of the grey stones that yet uplift themselves from amid the wreck of ages grow indistinct, like the picture upon which we look through the rolling years. Dimly those vestiges of habitations are seen, and dimly does the day when they were peopled present itself to our mental vision. But for imagination's aid it would be still more obscure, and when we remember that, notwithstanding the foundations are firm upon which we build, the superstructure is but the creation of fancy, we feel how little we really know concerning that long past time.

Quietude reigns over the waste, and the shadows slowly lengthen. Far away in the West the sky is filled with a golden radiance, but the heathery hills near by are growing dark. On the heath is a tall menhir, its form sharply defined against the ruddy glow. As it was to the patriarchs of old, so it is to us now. It is a pillar of witness — a witness that those who reared it looked above the earth on which they trod. Looked upward and found a hope, as we may do to-day, for it is a finger that points from that which perishes, and where the day becomes spent, and loses itself in darkness, to a kingdom of light that shall endure for ever.

* * *